Praise for *Bootstrapping Your Business*

"*Bootstrapping Your Business* will fill your cup with vision, inspiration, and practical tips on the art of bootstrapping. While many Americans think that its business heart and philosophy lies in the high-tech centers of Silicon Valley and Massachusetts, the truth is that the vast majority of businesses are started on small sums of bootstrapped cash—and that America's true heart lies in places like Bozeman, Montana."

—Rich Karlgaard, Publisher, *Forbes* magazine

"*Bootstrapping Your Business* speaks to the essence of entrepreneurship. Many entrepreneurs believe that they have to run amok trying to raise money. Sticking to building your product and then going out and selling it produces money, customers, and success. As a former CEO and a mentor to entrepreneurs, I knew I had a 'guts and brains' entrepreneur as opposed to a wanna-be when I saw he was bootstrapping RightNow."

—Rob Ryan, Founder, Ascend Communications; Founder, Entrepreneur America

"The best money comes from customers, not investors. That is a recurring theme in Greg Gianforte's terrific *Bootstrapping Your Business*. Selling a product or service early in the life of a company provides great feedback *and* the cash needed to refine the idea. Every entrepreneurial venture—indeed, every company— could benefit from this simple but powerful insight. Too often ventures raise lots of money, spend it as though if were 'free,' and never get the customer feedback that all Bootstrappers are forced to collect and respond to. Gianforte also provides real insight into fundamental business processes like selling, guerrilla marketing, and customer service. This book should be required reading for all entrepreneurs!"

—Professor Bill Sahlman, Harvard Business School

Praise for *Bootstrapping Your Business*

"*Bootstrapping Your Business* is filled with great insights on how to start and grow a highly successful business on very little capital even in a remote place like Bozeman, Montana. Every would-be entrepreneur should read this book for its fresh ideas and unique perspective."

—Thomas Weisel, CEO, Thomas Weisel Partners

"*Bootstrapping Your Business* is incredible! This is the most practical read that I've had in a while. However, I must say it is causing me great angst. I find myself wondering if I'm missing an opportunity out there. Within the first 20 pages, I was formulating product ideas."

—Mary Wardley, VP, IDC

"An accomplished serial entrepreneur, Greg Gianforte shares his story—and many others' collected through his work with Marcus Gibson—of applying the 'bootstrapping' philosophy to achieve long-term personal and financial success. 'Bootstrapping' may have only recently caught on in Silicon Valley, but it's a time-tested business approach that Greg and the other wily entrepreneurs profiled here have used in building great companies and great teams. Greg's most recent creation, RightNow Technologies, is a terrific example of how this philosophy can lead to great commercial results, personal fulfillment, and even a wildly successful IPO."

—Paul Chamberlain, Managing Director, Morgan Stanley; Member, Forbes Midas List

BOOTSTRAPPING
YOUR BUSINESS

Start and Grow a Successful Company
with Almost No Money

Greg Gianforte
with Marcus Gibson

Adams Media
Avon, Massachusetts

Published by
Adams Media, an F+W Publications Company
57 Littlefield Street, Avon, MA 02322. U.S.A.
www.adamsmedia.com

ISBN: 1-59337-387-2

Printed in the United States of America.

J   I   H   G   F   E   D   C   B   A

Library of Congress Cataloging-in-Publication Data
Gianforte, Greg.
Bootstrapping your business / Greg Gianforte with Marcus Gibson.
p.   cm.
ISBN 1-59337-387-2
1. New business enterprises. I. Gibson, Marcus. II. Title.

HD62.5.G52 2005
658.1'1—dc22

2005002133

This book is available at quantity discounts for bulk purchases.
For information, please call 1-800-872-5627.

CONTENTS

Acknowledgments . . . . **vii**

Foreword . . . . **ix**
The Death of Distance—Long Predicted, Finally Here
by Rich Karlgaard, Publisher, Forbes *magazine*

Introduction . . . . **.xv**
Meet the Bootstrappers—and Join Them

Chapter 1 . . . . **1**
It All Starts with a Blank Piece of Paper

Chapter 2 . . . . **17**
Make Sales Job Number One

Chapter 3 . . . . **31**
The Nuts and Bolts of Selling

Chapter 4 . . . . **45**
There Is *Always* Another Way

Chapter 5 . . . . **59**
Scarcity Is Good: The Art of Thrift

Chapter 6 . . . . **69**
Managing That Precious Cash

Chapter 7 . . . . **89**
Getting Paid and Finding Finance and Credit

Chapter 8 . . . . **99**
Start Small; Think Big

Chapter 9 111
Marketing on a Shoestring

Chapter 10. 129
Making the Press Work for You

Chapter 11. 149
Stress-Busting Strategies

Chapter 12. 165
Hiring the Right People at the Right Time

Chapter 13. 187
You Live or Die by Your Customer Service

Chapter 14. 205
Act Like a Winner

Appendix. 215
The Bootstrapper's Toolbox

Index 227

ACKNOWLEDGMENTS

W hen we first sat down and began researching the concept of Bootstrapping, little did we know just how far-reaching the phenomenon had become. From the outset, we were inundated with epic tales from dozens of dedicated Bootstrappers. We would like to extend our grateful thanks to all those who gave unstintingly of their time.

In particular, a small number of visionary individuals from across the country have helped us document and map out the ideas and functions of Bootstrapping. These include Tim Jenkins, of the consultancy Point B Solutions in Seattle; Lurita Doan, of New Technology Management Inc. in Washington, D.C.; Sean Murphy, cofounder of Canvas Systems in Atlanta; Paul Szydlowski, of Prime Valet in Cincinnati; Joseph Lahoud, of LC Technologies in Fairfax, Virginia; Jon Nordmark, CEO of eBags.com, the online luggage business in Denver; Andrew Field of PrintingForLess.com in Livingston, Montana; and Lon McGowan, founder of the iClick digital camera business in Seattle.

A special thanks must go to Michelle N. Dimarob, the information guru at the National Federation of Independent Businesses, who kindly offered us a list of mightily Bootstrapped

businesses. We also are grateful to the many reporters, researchers, and editors who steered us toward examples of successful
Bootstrappers; a particular thanks goes to John Cook, business
reporter at *The Seattle Post-Intelligencer.*

We would like to express our gratitude to the staff of coauthor
Greg Gianforte's own Bootstrapped company, RightNow Technologies in Bozeman, Montana, with special thanks to Rob Irizarry
for his insights into customer service; to Susan Carstensen, the
CFO; to Kim Scurry for her views on experimental marketing;
and to Brady Meltzer, Marcus Bragg, and Mike Myer for their
contributions to the chapters on sales techniques.

Marcus Gibson, the coauthor, would like to thank Greg and
his wife, Susan, and RightNow's press officer Alison Piper for
their hospitality during the time he spent in Bozeman explor-
ing and researching the concept of Bootstrapping. It is doubtful
that the people of Bozeman realize they have in their modest-
size town such a dynamic group of people whose ideas and can-
do spirit have chalked up a real achievement—one similar to
those accomplished by motivated Bootstrappers in towns and cities across America. Our goal in writing this book is to put the
concept of Bootstrapping onto the economic pedestal it deserves,
and to give readers the information and inspiration they need to
join the ranks of these successful Bootstrapping pioneers.

Greg Gianforte
Marcus Gibson

The Death of Distance— Long Predicted, Finally Here

Technology's spread into the American boondocks is great news for Bootstrappers. Opportunities to create cutting-edge businesses are limited only by the imagination, not by geography. Once you get rid of distance as a constraint, America's heartland, the home to companies like coauthor Greg Gianforte's RightNow Technologies, provides many advantages dear to the heart of Bootstrappers: lower costs, highly educated and dedicated workforces, civic support, and so on.

The success of Greg's hi-tech start-up in Bozeman, Montana, a thousand miles away from Silicon Valley, isn't an anomaly. America is rapidly becoming a broadband nation, closing the technology gap between large and small places. Broadband penetration grew rapidly even during the economically lousy years of 2001 to 2003, partly fueled by the growth of telecommuters and home-based businesses. Almost anybody in a town with a population of more than 25,000 can get broadband service within days of making the call to the local phone company or ISP. Rural areas are next.

Technology is only going to get better. The most efficient and productive place to hold a meeting in the twenty-first century is right on your desktop. Video desktop conferencing services such as WebEx, allow you to do just that—work remotely and communicate easily with others who are thousands of miles away. It's also not uncommon for businesses to use Instant Messaging to communicate with clients and coworkers in real time. Thus Bootstrappers needn't spend so much of their two most valuable resources—time and money—traveling on airplanes.

Bootstrapping Your Business will fill your cup with vision, inspiration, and practical tips on the art of Bootstrapping. Let me give you one tip of my own before you move on to the main event of Greg and Marcus's text.

As communications technologies evolve, more American Bootstrappers can engage in what I call "Geographic Arbitrage." It works like this:

1. You start a business in a small city or town and keep your costs way down.
2. But you get paid as if you're in a big city.

This is increasingly possible. Say you want to start a software, financial, or marketing business. You decide to shake off the costly coastal urban infrastructure and relocate to a cheaper rural region. But you maintain your ties to the larger urban area and charge the same fees or prices you charged when you lived in Profligate Corners. In other words, you harvest your dollars from Silicon Valley, Seattle, New York, London, and Tokyo, but you spend and invest them in Boise or Bozeman.

Congratulations! You are a true twenty-first-century Bootstrapper! You are a Geographic Arbitrageur! Thanks to computers, the Internet, FedEx, cell phones, and so on, you can do this.

Not everyone is cut out to be a Geographic Arbitrageur, of course. It takes buckets of moxie and self-motivation to work hours (or even time zones) away from the main arenas. It takes a certain knowledge and sophistication about how the main arenas operate. I have seen some professionals play the GeoArb game without ever having lived in the economic powerhouses, but it's rare. It helps enormously to have lived on the urban coasts, put in a few years, met people in your field face-to-face, and established a professional reputation and a contact list.

Suppose you lost your high-paying white-collar job in a big city. What would you do? File for unemployment? Probably not. Show up at a bogus "jobs-retraining" program and be taught by a social worker who knows diddly-squat about the way business really works? No. In all likelihood you'd set up a home office and try your hand as a consultant. That's what 150,000 Americans have done since 2000.

Drew Massey, a New York magazine entrepreneur, recently moved back to Denver and sent me this e-mail:

> Although I am a media entrepreneur at heart, I have always longed to return to my home state of Colorado. Life is very good. Nice to have a 102-year-old, 2,600-square-foot house for the price of a one-bedroom apartment in Harlem. Not to mention saving enough money on my monthly parking bill to buy a vintage '55 T-Bird to put into my four-car garage. Even splurged on the rights to four season tickets to the Broncos—a 10-minute walk from my house. Rockies baseball is a 5-minute bike ride (joked with my buddies to try that in the Bronx). Ditto for Avalanche hockey and the famous lively LoDo [lower downtown Denver] scene. Airport is 30 minutes door-to-door (no tunnels, no O'Hare or [San Francisco] highways). And the best benefit is the access to my favorite skiing. Casually leave at 8:30 on a weekday (after checking the 7:30 market opening and reading the *Wall Street Journal*) and I'm on the chairlift by 10:00. Tell me again why I should be packed like a sardine on the 4/5/6 or 1/3/9 subway in New York City?
>
> P.S. I kept my NYC cell phone to fool everyone.

Drew is not unique. Five years ago, if you wanted to be in the middle of the most lucrative opportunities, you had to be in one of the great urban centers. No longer. Suddenly, smart and ambitious entrepreneurs like Drew Massey can set up shop wherever there's a high-speed Net connection. A number of experts such as Joel Kotkin, author of *The New Geography,* have identified an emerging tech industry in parts of the country that provide lifestyle opportunities to knowledge workers.

This "hidden tech" movement, a term coined by author Amy Zuckerman, refers to a clustering of like-minded tech professionals far removed from urban environments. Zuckerman writes that the hidden tech economy includes hard-core "techies"—software programmers or hardware developers—but also lawyers, patent agents, jewelry retailers, management trainers, content providers, graphic artists, Web designers, and marketing specialists. They might be professional telecommuters, freelancers playing the GeoArb game, or Bootstrappers who develop and sell products or services from a home or small office and leverage the Web to expand their reach.

The "hidden" portion has two meanings. Sometimes, as in the case of home offices squirreled away in a spare bedroom, den, or attic, they are literally hidden from sight. More often, though, they are hidden from government, private sector, or academic statisticians because many are not incorporated. That means they might not be captured by any government reporting service.

Ranging in age from their twenties to postretirement, these Hidden Techsters are developing operations that might be small financially, but are potent in terms of the alliances and contacts they maintain worldwide. And these Hidden Techsters are boosting the economies of the regions where they are relocating to, because they have the means to purchase high-end homes; require a wide variety of technological and professional services; hire subcontractors, part-timers, and even full-time employees;

and often create alliances that help keep other regional cottage companies and service professionals afloat.

There are dozens of these hidden tech economies tucked away throughout America, many like the one where Zuckerman lives in west-central Massachusetts. This region draws talent and inspiration from the five colleges and many prep schools that permeate the region. Lots of students from New York or Boston chose to settle here rather than seek opportunities back home.

Daniel Pink, in his book *Free Agent Nation,* counts at least 18 million Americans who are sole proprietors or operating their own small, home-based companies. He believes this is just the beginning of a significant trend toward self-employment. The Great Bust (predicted by author Daniel Arnold as the greatest depression in American and United Kingdom history, to start around 2012) and the subsequent export of white-collar jobs to India and Asia can only accelerate this trend.

While many Americans think that its business heart and philosophy lies in the hi-tech centers of Silicon Valley and Massachusetts, the truth is that the vast majority of businesses are started on small sums of Bootstrapped cash—and that America's true heart lies in places like Bozeman, Montana.

Rich Karlgaard
Publisher, *Forbes* magazine

Meet the Bootstrappers— and Join Them

Before we introduce many of the Bootstrappers whose stories of success you'll hear about later in this book, let's answer one very basic question: "What is Bootstrapping?"

Simply put, *Bootstrapping* is the act of starting a business with little or no external funding. Even though hundreds of thousands of Americans start businesses each year this way, few realize that they are members of a silent, yet enormous economic subcommunity—the "Bootstrapper" section of the economy. The art of building a business with little or no money is by far the most common way Americans build businesses, but we believe we're the first to codify in detail the art of Bootstrapping

In this book, you will find the core advice and step-by-step information you need to start and sustain your business. We give an easy-to-follow road map for students, executives, seniors, and entrepreneurs alike who are keen to apply their talents and imagination to the world of business.

Much of the advice contained in "How To" business books is of no value to the Bootstrapper. Similarly, training schemes and formal business school education mostly focus on skills such as writing business plans and ways of attracting venture capital funding. This information is often of little value to the 98 percent of start-up professionals who begin businesses in America each year without a cent in venture capital funding. If you've attended a business school, you might want to forget many of the priorities and approaches you were taught. Those lengthy business plans, money-raising exercises, and exotic marketing reports are designed to serve the interests of large corporations, big management consultancies, venture capital firms, and government grant organizations with deep pockets. They are academic in nature, and impractical in business. Books and courses have rarely concentrated on the core, day-to-day skills that a Bootstrapper needs to know. Bootstrapping is simply in a different league—sometimes it seems like a different universe.

You will read here about an extraordinary cross section of Bootstrapping Americans, all of whom are tough, determined, realistic, and thoroughly human in their approach to business. Open-minded and contemptuous of conventional thinking and petty regulation, these Bootstrappers are keen to take advice, maximize their opportunities, and build for the long term.

Let's meet some of the people behind these Bootstrapping success stories:

- Lon McGowan, who at the age of twenty-two used a pocketful of credit cards, a low-cost publicity stunt, and a clever shift in marketing strategy to jump-start iClick, is now a highly successful Seattle business selling low-cost digital cameras.
- Lurita Doan, who began her company, New Technology Management Inc. in 1990 in Washington, D.C., after her employer turned her down for a project because she was "not management material." Her company now has revenues of $200 million, employs more than 150 people, and is at the forefront of U.S. border surveillance and IT services. Lurita is one of the most successful African-American businesswomen of her generation.

- Mark Peltier, from St. Paul, Minnesota, who designed and patented his own aroma machine. It was his sixth business venture. Starting out in 1983, his company Aromasys has now installed "sweet-air" units in most of the hotels and casinos in Las Vegas, and most recently at the giant new airport in Hong Kong.

- Jon Nordmark, founder of the online luggage business eBags.com in Denver, put everything he had on the line to found his company in 1998, and, after suffering through a deep downturn in 2001, bounced back to sell more than one million bags in 2003.

- Andrew Field, who decided to focus on what his customers really wanted and valued, changed the name of his business to the easy-to-grasp PrintingForLess.com, and was able to build the nation's leading online printing business from the small rural town of Livingston, Montana.

- Sean Murphy, cofounder of Canvas Systems, a reseller of refurbished computer equipment in Atlanta, is "The King of Thrift." He instills his penny-pinching strategies in a workforce that has grown from four to 250 with no outside financing.

- Joseph Lahoud, who started the engineering business LC Technologies in Fairfax, Virginia. During the rough early days, his staff once collectively walked into his office and said that their best advice was to close the business. He didn't, and they stayed. Months later, after the business became a success, his staff told him they didn't leave because "we just couldn't leave you there working by yourself."

- Tim Jenkins, cofounder of the consulting group Point B Solutions in Seattle, whose company treats its loyal and dedicated employees in a way that is a model of corporate HR practice.

- Paul Szydlowski, of Prime Valet Cleaners in Cincinnati, whose creative niche marketing campaigns and constant consideration of his customers' needs have turned his company from one modest dry-cleaning establishment in 1990 into a five-store, $2-million business today.

These are just some of the successful Bootstrappers you will meet in the following pages. In defining and describing Boot-strapping, we have deliberately focused on the key points that apply to *all* businesses. It does not matter if your business is a small, low-tech venture building a craft-based product of modest value, or if you are the originator of a hi-tech business, striving for big returns on a process that took a great deal of private R&D funds to roll out. In any business, it is the very first few steps in starting out that are some of the toughest. This book will help you tackle those obstacles with skill and confidence, and it will also teach you to concentrate on the core fundamentals of run-ning the business.

The National Federation of Independent Business (NFIB) estimates that small businesses represent over 99 percent of all employers in America, and even more important, that small busi-nesses creates 80 percent of all new jobs in America. The unstop-pable urge among Americans to start their own businesses shows no sign of slowing down. The crucial point is that the majority of small businesses are started with tiny, sometimes laughably tiny, amounts of cash. Many of our Bootstrappers began with $100. In October 2002, *Inc.* magazine, which follows the pat-terns of American entrepreneurship closely, noted that 14 per-cent of its 500 fastest-growing companies had opened with less than $1,000. According to the Wells Fargo/NFIB Series on busi-ness start-ups, 70 percent of small business owners started with less than $20,000.

Experience shows that there are Entrepreneurs, there are Innovators, and then there are Bootstrappers. We believe Boot-strappers are America's true unidentified entrepreneurial heroes. In our research, we have discovered some extraordinary stories of

innovation, risk taking, energy, passion, pain, and, above all, tri-
umphs against a series of seemingly unconquerable barriers.

Reading the stories in this book, you might be surprised by
the quality and sheer variety of the ideas that have been turned
into sustainable businesses. No business activity is off-limits to
the bands of Bootstrappers who are introducing new products
and processes across the nation. The NFIB says, "Most ideas
for businesses originate from other work or hobbies; sometimes
the ideas are related to educational courses, chance happen-
ings, or suggestions."

Why are so many people becoming Bootstrappers? As big
companies continue to downsize, the attractions of working for a
large firm have sharply declined in recent years. Even the prospect of a proper pension has often disappeared. By contrast, working in a small but innovative company holds out the prospect of
a good income, control over your own affairs, the opportunity to
build a first-rate team, and the challenge of starting something
new or even unique. For a fortunate few, there is the very real
prospect of making a well-deserved fortune.

For most Bootstrappers, this is unlikely to happen in their
first business. But as several case studies in this book show,
serial Bootstrappers enjoy a heightened degree of success as their
skills and acumen improve. It is startling to remember just how
recently some of America's biggest businesses were started. Dell
Computer began in 1984—"with $1,000 and an unprecedented
idea—to build relationships with customers," states his biogra-
phy. Microsoft was launched in 1975. In 2005, Dell is destined
to become a $50 billion business; for the full fiscal year of 2004,
Microsoft notched up revenues of $36.8 billion. Both were started
on a shoestring, without external funding.

Much of what you read in this book will run directly contrary
to the conventional education at business schools, and will be at
odds with the advice of business start-up organizations, a host of

mentors, "experienced" financiers, and big company executives. Conventional wisdom demands that you write a comprehensive business plan, often running to dozens of pages, as a prerequisite to getting started. Our advice: forget what you've taught, and start with a clean slate.

Greg Gianforte, coauthor of this book, is a serial entrepreneur and the founder of the software firm RightNow Technologies in Bozeman, Montana. He built a $60 million business by following the principles and practices of Bootstrapping. Through his experience and that of hundreds of others, we believe that Bootstrapping is the best way to start a new business. Here are just some of the reasons why starting on your own as a lean and mean Bootstrapper is better than taking the more conventional route and relying on outside funding:

1. Bootstrapping is the quickest and surest way of building a solid business. Why? Because you are forced to deal with customers and fulfill their needs from day one. This compels you to maximize your efforts on sales, and to meet the real needs of real customers. If you had plenty of external funding, you might be fooled into thinking you had created a business. Not true. You have a business only when you have paying customers. Remember: "No sales equals zero business."

2. Having lots of cash only delays the onset of the sales learning process. Selling is the hardest job of all. You have to learn it quickly and thoroughly, and then teach others to do it quickly and thoroughly. Excess cash on day one only delays the day when you have to screw up your courage, pick up the phone—and ask for that First Order. Only then will you discover if you have the basis of a business.

3. Few Bootstrappers waste money; but most can make it. If you had $100,000 or $1 million in funding, what would you do? Leave it in the bank? No, you'd go out and spend it—which is the last thing you should do. You'd spend it and waste it long before you'd build a viable business. Getting a big check from a finance house does not create a real business with real customers, real products and services, and real profits. It creates an artificial business, a castle in the air, a "virtual entity," at best. If you have venture capital money, you will be forced to spend it. You won't be an entrepreneur; in truth you'll be little more than a fund-raiser.

4. Bootstrapping doesn't waste time. You can start your business immediately. It could be this morning or this afternoon—you choose. But with external funding, "they" choose for you. Venture capital firms might take up to a year or more to decide on whether to invest. They might want a 200-page business plan; their activities might force you to spend up to $50,000 in professional fees. Entrepreneurs spend an inordinate amount of time trying to find sources of external funding—when they should really be out there searching for customers.

5. Bootstrapping means you can't make a fatal financial mistake early on in your business. This is simple: Because a Bootstrapper has no money, it's not possible for him or her to make a costly, mortal error in spending it.

6. Bootstrapping is the lowest risk technique of starting a company. Starting with no money means you don't need to provide collateral, so there is no risk to the family home or core savings if things go awry.

7. A Bootstrapper will own much, if not all, of what he or she creates, in contrast to clients of external finance. Jon Nordmark, founder of eBags.com, says: "A VC-backed company needs to double before the founders benefit. In down-rounds, the founders are wiped out. Many VCs take preferred stock, and the founders only have ordinary shares. In a liquidation, they'd get very little." Starting out with little or no money means that if you should succeed you are very likely to own all or a substantial portion of your enterprise. You will also keep control of your entity. In time, you can develop it further, sell it, or give it to your children.

8. A Bootstrapper starts out with independence and freedom of action. You are not dependent upon the whims of any third parties—banks, grant agencies, or finance houses—you are dependent only upon your customers. But if you take external funding, you become the slave of the business plan.

9. Having no money forces unconventional thinking. Necessity truly is the mother of invention, and a lack of resources forces Bootstrappers to think outside the box. Innovative and often better ideas result.

Successful Bootstrappers are among the most multitalented and adventurous people of our generation. The achievement of creating and sustaining a business based on sales and little external funding is a terrific achievement. If there were Olympic awards for business, the successful Bootstrapper would win the gold medal. Why not become one of them?

And if you can you think of more good reasons to Bootstrap a business, let us know. We'd very much like to hear from readers about their thoughts and business experiences in the months and years to come. More than anything, we would like to look back on this book in decades ahead and find that thousands of good people became Bootstrappers after they read it. Please feel free to contact us at our special Bootstrapper's Web site: *www.BootstrapIt.com.* Welcome to the Honorable Profession of the Bootstrapper!

CHAPTER 1

IT ALL STARTS WITH A BLANK PIECE OF PAPER

"One doesn't discover new lands without consenting
to lose sight of the shore for a very long time."

—*André Gide*

I n 1997, the highly successful company RightNow Technologies started when Greg Gianforte, coauthor of this book, wrote down on a single piece of paper a list of features he thought customers might want from a new piece of software. From that moment onward, the die was cast.

Do you want to start your own business? Well, then take out your own pencil and paper. Use a pencil, because there will be lots of additions and rubbings out. Write down your initial offering—your first outline of what you could offer a waiting market, together with its principal features and elements.

Your next step is to start calling some prospective customers and asking them what they like or don't like about your idea. Would they be willing to buy it? Is there a mismatch between your offering and their requirements? Yes, almost certainly. After you've called ten—or fifty—prospective customers, you will have gained an unrivaled, in-depth, up-to-the-minute portrait of your market's needs. Keep that piece of paper. You might want to frame it later, because it's the first and probably the most important item in your company's archive.

You Don't Need a Product to Sell It

At first reading, this statement might seem impossible. But once Bootstrappers grasp its essential truth, they realize it's their biggest single advantage. One must have a product to start a business, surely? Think again. Conventional thinking would have you believe that unless you have a product, preferably polished and very complete, you have no business. In fact the very opposite is true. For the Bootstrapper nothing could be worse than having an existing product or service when customers invariably want Something Completely Different.

This is your biggest advantage—though you won't know it yet. Having no money, no staff, no equipment, and above all, no product is a tremendous bonus to a Bootstrapper. Why? There are dozens of good reasons, so here are just a few:

1. You are forced to produce the product or service that the customer wants, and wants most. It won't be the product you were craving to sell them—it'll be the product they're craving to buy.

2. You can't lose out. If no one in the world buys your offering, the Bootstrapper parts with nothing but some time and a phone bill. Your slim resources are all still available for your next idea or for an amended product.

3. The process of Bootstrapping is nothing less than the fastest and most efficient way of telling you whether you have a sound product and a strong basis for a business.

4. It compels you to be creative. Only an open mind, applied imagination, and a good listening ear will get you to where you want to go. Bootstrapping is the purest and clearest of test beds for your business idea.

5. It is the best opportunity to build the sort of business that makes America tick. Even better, if it's successful, you will own most or all of it. It could be your future "job for life," the ultimate security for you, your staff, family, and colleagues. You could finally be in full control of your own destiny—a goal for many a seasoned Bootstrapper. And because you have little to offer initially except a modest wage and a great future, you are likely to attract only the hardiest, most courageous, and enterprising people as employees.

Eight Strategies for Successful Bootstrapping

No matter what sort of business you're seeking to start, here are the strategies you'll need to follow to become a successful Bootstrapper.

Strategy #1: Find the Right Product or Service

There is one question you have to be able to answer before any other: How are you going to make some *real* money out of this? This is important. The world is full of modest, mediocre low-margin opportunities across each and every business sector. In complete contrast, the clever Bootstrapper should search assiduously for that special, high-margin pot of gold. It's not easy to find: Only by talking to customers will you begin to discover such an opportunity. The key is to prove, beyond doubt, that there is a strong market for your product and service, and crucially, that customers are prepared to pay for it. Try to get your operations going quickly by learning how to do as many tasks yourself as you

a bootstrapper's tale:

Give the People What They Really Want

ootstrappers can change the face of whole industries. Take Montana printer Andrew Field. Finding something new in the 500-year-old world of printing is far from easy. Not long ago, nearly all companies employed full-time print buyers and an army of finicky designers to produce brochures and other corporate literature. They had a choice of 3,000 different types of paper, and they always insisted on seeing physical proofs of the materials before signing the order. But this costly and complicated process excluded many millions of small businesses that couldn't afford these prices, and had little idea of how to design their own brochures.

Step forward Andrew Field, a professional printer with a dozen years of experience. Back in 1996, Andrew's print firm was struggling to find extra accounts. He'd called every business in the state with little success. With the advent of the Web, he searched for ways of making the market not more complex, but simpler. In eight short years Andrew's print business, operating from the small town of Livingston in rural Montana, has become a world leader in online printing. Today it holds America's largest database of commercial print customers, a staggering 17 million. His sales in 2004 reached $17 million, growing at a rate of 40 percent a year. How did this single-minded Bootstrapper achieve it in just eight short years?

First, he asked a friend to write some software that enabled his Web site to accept the graphic designs that had been developed in the mainstream creative design package Microsoft Publisher. Most designs

4

were created on Apple Mac computers, and many print systems were incompatible with Publisher. Next, he set up a temporary Web site for each customer so they could preview their print item. Realizing that most small companies wanted their printing in two or three days rather than the industry standard of two or three weeks, he offered his customers just four types of paper, which met almost everyone's needs. Then he waited. And waited. Andrew knew his Web service was bold and unique—so why weren't people banging on his door? The Web site was named ExpressColor.com, and the silence was deafening. Sensing his error, Andrew changed the name to PrintingForLess.com (PFL), and small businesses began calling by the tens of thousands.

As a dedicated Bootstrapper who listened to his customers, Andrew didn't offer any guarantee on color matching—one of the hallowed rituals of conventional printing. "Few customers really cared," he says. "What they did care about was easy access to real-time instant pricing, instant file-uploading, auto-payment, and online proofing services." Customer testimonials poured in. Today, one out of four new orders comes via the recommendation of a happy client. After each job, PFL sends out a personal e-mail to the client, offering suggestions on how they can better prepare files or produce more attractive designs. "We provide a Nordstrom level of customer service for a Wal-Mart price," he said. "Our success has been a function of the service being offered—not just that it can be accessed online." Best of all, customers paid via credit card and in advance, so cash flow was secure. Ten plants across the United States currently produce the finished works. "Our real success is ahead of us," says Andrew. In a single sweep, the Bootstrapper from Livingston presumed to transform the printing world—a $100 billion-a-year industry in the United States alone—and has succeeded.

can—or, best of all, by figuring out what you *don't* have to do at all. Identify those quick, break-even, cash-generating products, the especially higher-value items that can be sold through personal selling methods.

Strategy #2: Immerse Yourself

Whatever your start-up method, the long sequence of phone calls to prospective customers must be a truly immersive process. This activity is the bedrock of all Bootstrapping. Only through this deep and instructive experience will you find that elusive business opportunity. For the true Bootstrapper the real learning doesn't start until you have "live" customers. So the goal of the Bootstrapper must be to source a real customer as rapidly as possible. The learning does not truly start until you do it full-time, and the whole Bootstrapping process is one of constant investigation.

Suppose you're considering a start-up company offering corporate cleaning services. Do a little basic research. Get the brochures of existing companies, and read them thoroughly. Call their key customers and ask them what they like or don't like about their existing service supplier. If all of the customers are delighted with the service—which is unlikely—move on to a new market segment. It could be that all of the owners of big offices are happy, but the midmarket is distinctly unhappy. In that case, direct your efforts to the middle market exclusively.

The immersion process for someone considering a different type of business—providing home meals, for example—is very similar. He or she also must determine who the key target customers are most likely to be. Are they busy executives who can't leave their desks at lunchtime? Are they nurses at local hospitals who might be dissatisfied with cafeteria food? Or maybe the cafeteria is good, but it closes at 6 P.M., which means that nurses coming off shifts at 7 P.M. are hungry but can't find a decent meal in the area. The Bootstrapper should be asking, "Where's the biggest latent opportunity here?"

One possible strategy: Ask the hospital managers this: "May I ring the wards each evening at around 6:30 P.M. to ask if any nurses want a meal waiting for them the moment they arrive home?" Could this be the start of a regular supply of meals to a grateful market? It certainly could be—but the classic Bootstrapper has not yet cooked a single meal. If all of the city hospitals are overjoyed with the catering facilities, don't stop there. Try other twenty-four-hour workforce and night-shift locations, such as airports, bus stations, and manufacturing plants.

Strategy #3: Become the Expert Yourself

Beware of "experts." Instead, become the expert yourself in your chosen niche. In the same way that market researchers impose a barrier between you and your future customers, a long list of "experts" can have the same, highly damaging impact on your business—and also cost you dearly in professional fees in the process. A whole raft of analysts, advisers, consultants, sector experts, failed middle-ranking managers of long extinct companies, and part-time university professors will be happy to fulfill this role. But in the end the effect is the same: They increase the distance between the Bootstrapper and his or her market. Nothing can be more fatal to a business than a supposed "expert's" intervention.

Obviously, some experts can provide you with good advice, but very few will do it for free. At best, most experts are simply relating secondhand knowledge. In turn, this knowledge is often derived from third-party sources such as analyst reports, and rarely from direct contact with customers. Worse still, this flood of trend watching is frequently inaccurate and based on the suppositions of "expert" analysts. Sadly, many of these analysts are often only a few years out of college and have no work experience in the sector concerned.

a bootstrapper's tale:

Giving Birth to a New Business

Back in 1990, Lurita Doan, a thirty-one-year-old African-American woman, was told by her employer that she was not going to be appointed manager on a new project because she wasn't "management material." Furious, she started her own IT services business. Inching forward from one small job for government agencies after another, she worked alone for three years. She was so hard up for cash she often walked from her home in the Washington, D.C., suburbs rather than pay for public transport.

Walking door-to-door between government offices, she endlessly asked if she could do any IT jobs. She made visits as sharply dressed as any CEO, answered the phone as her assistant, and then made lightning changes into overalls in the ladies room—and became the faceless contract technician. "To appear much bigger, I'd say 'I'll have to check with management about that,'" she recalls. Luckily, her skills with Unix made her a desirable commodity. Lurita particularly excelled in resurrecting dead IT systems. "I was often their last-gasp hope," she says.

Her big break came when she was heavily pregnant with her second child. Business had dropped sharply after the agencies became increasingly afraid of insurance claims as a result of any "falls or slips" she might have during her pregnancy. Then, by chance, the U.S. Navy was unable to make a $150-million IT system work, and it could find no one who could. But somebody thought they "knew somebody who could"—that somebody turned out to be Lurita. It was an IT system for an aircraft carrier, and she was forty-one weeks pregnant. Lurita worked for two whole days at Navy HQ and breathed life into the gray cabinets. A few days later, they called again. "We now need you to install it—on the carrier. Can you do this for us, please? *Please*?" With an ambulance waiting at the dockside to take her to the hospital if necessary, Lurita went aboard the carrier at Norfolk naval base in Virginia, and after a mammoth session, got the job done.

Delighted and grateful, the Navy put the word around: "If there are any jobs going, give them to this lady." Not long afterward, she landed her first $1-million contract. Today, her company NMTI (New Technology Management, Inc.) is a leader in border surveillance technology for the U.S. government, with a turnover of more than $200 million. Lurita, who still owns 100 percent of her company, passed on another tradition. NMTI is known for having a very high birthrate among the employees and their families.

Lurita's ten best tips for a budding Bootstrapper are:

1. Recruit desperate and grateful customers.

2. Don't be disheartened by rude and dismissive reactions during sales calls. The best time to make a sales call is right after the worst, nastiest rejection—because at that time the next call *can't* be nearly as bad as the last.

3. Grow with your customers. Spot up-and-coming managers in the organization and try to grow with them. Don't always start at the top.

4. Help your suppliers in your own supply chain, because this will benefit everybody.

5. Offer your first customers their money back if your solution doesn't work.

6. Be brutally honest about your business model. Bootstrappers should not become empire builders, but should expand only to where profits can be made.

7. Think far ahead into your business market, searching for gaps, needs, and opportunities.

8. Make a full-time effort to start up your business. Many people dream about starting a business at the same time they're working a day job. "Oh, I'll do it in the evening," they tell themselves. Sadly, there are few examples where this has worked.

9. Don't bother writing a three-year business plan because it's virtually useless. A Bootstrapper's Planning Horizon is—next week! That's the reality of running a small business. Contrary to all the dictates of business schools, running a business is very tactical, and not strategic.

10. Expect to everything to take three times as long as you predicted.

Worst of all, you will invariably find that these analysts are often ignorant of the true innovations that might be happening in your sector. Confucius said: "You are never in a position to learn unless you are totally confused." In the period spent searching for a valuable business opportunity it is easy to become mentally frustrated by the outpouring of often contradictory advice and information. And very often the consultants are just plain wrong.

The ardent Bootstrapper should avoid these advisers—and their fees—and go back to original sources in order to discover those priceless innovations that are going on underneath the veneer of paid-for information. Consultants will divert a lot of your time from the task of building the business. Get rid of them!

Strategy #4: Think in Black and White

The world is full of shades of gray, but to the time- and cash-constrained Bootstrapper, the world must be viewed only in black and white. Why? Because the range of distractions that are likely to impinge upon your busy day are many and varied. Learn to paint your business issues in primary colors—in order to keep it *simple*. Business schools make business sound complicated, but in reality all you need is a product or service that you can produce at a cost less than someone is willing to pay. It's not difficult, and the Bootstrapper has no time for endless complexity. He or she must concentrate exclusively on the core issues at the heart of the business, and must seek clarity in decision making at every turn.

Strategy #5: Get Ready for Rough Times Ahead

"No nickel, no gum," says Jon Nordmark, "that's what my mother's constant reminder during his youth. Mom's common sense is better than a Harvard degree." Jon, the founder of eBags. com, the now very successful online retailer of luggage and handbags in Denver, has had some nerve-wracking moments since the company was founded in May 1998. But he has never lost faith in his Bootstrapping skills. "Too much money makes you stupid," he says. "You have to live longer than the learning curve." Starting as he did before the dotcom era, he was emphatically refused funding. "More than 200 VCs said 'No,'" he says. The four founders worked for free until they managed to raise some cash. The first employee didn't get paid for two months. But Jon was determined. "If you have a big interest, you'll really strive to make it work. I had 'skin in the game.' If I lost, I'd lose everything." Jon had no wages for eight months, spent all of his $100,000 savings, built up debts of $60,000 on credit cards, and exhausted the $20,000 given to him by his parents. "I was putting it all on the line," he says. He remembers lying awake at night, thinking: "Well, if I lost everything tomorrow, they couldn't take very much as I haven't got anything left. At least I've got my dog!" To keep going, the founders organized "cash calls." "When we had a bill due," he recalls, "we'd all write a check to eBags." One of the founders walked out; he wouldn't pay. The three who stayed are still there today.

Strategy #6: *Don't* Buy an Existing Business

You'll discover many opportunities to buy all kinds of small businesses. Couples retire, or a big mall opens in the neighborhood and local shop owners want a way out. Even when there are no wrong reasons for buying a business, the Bootstrapper should exercise real caution. First and foremost, existing staff is used to running the business their way, which is usually much more relaxed than the business hothouse you envisage. Second, it is supremely difficult to plant Bootstrapping techniques into the various cozy cliques and mafias that flourish inside many conventional small firms.

Just in case you still think you can easily buy a business that can be run the way you want and need it to be, consider the experience of this highly successful Bootstrapper. Paul Szydlowski was keen to expand his single Prime Valet dry-cleaning store in Cincinnati, so he found another dry-cleaning business owned by a husband-and-wife team. The books looked good and the location was excellent. The deal was done.

Then the problems began. "It was a very loose operation," Paul remembers. There was no time clock in the office and staff often brought in their own washing and their friends' washing, and spent a lot of company time on that rather than performing profitable duties. "One day I saw a dozen bridesmaid's dresses—and I was told it was 'being done for a friend,'" says Paul. "I'd had enough." He decided to rebuild the business from scratch. No more free dry cleaning for friends, and all staff functions such as payroll and accounts payable had to be handled by line positions. Money had to be taken to the bank on Fridays without exception. These mild-sounding measures caused a mutiny at the main plant, recalls Paul. "It was clear that introducing a new culture into the old regime was going to be difficult." Within twelve months, fourteen out of fifteen staff were replaced, but by the time the last one left, the business was highly efficient and cleaning 1,000 shirts per day. For the Bootstrapper the lesson is a hard one: It is often best to cherry-pick your staff and then teach them the practices and principles of Bootstrapping as part of a new and fresh corporate entity.

Strategy #7: Consider Carefully Before Joining Up with a Partner

Dealing with business partners can be frustrating and irksome. When partners disagree the entire business suffers and often fails. People, even those you have known for a long, long time, have an odd way of becoming just plain weird—unrealistic, unreasonable, conspiratorial, lazy, and even greedy—once they become your business partner. They turn into people you think you never met. So be extremely careful in picking business partners!

If you do decide to start a business with a partner, here are some things you can do to protect yourself.

1. Establish up front before you start the business how someone will leave the business. For example, you might agree that if someone leaves in the first two years he or she gets nothing, or perhaps some small percentage of the last twelve months of sales paid out over time. The percentage might be higher if the business has had a profit. If you leave these discussions till your separation discussion, disagreements will be extremely difficult if not impossible to resolve.

2. If you have multiple partners, decide how you will resolve disputes. This is especially important for an even number of partners in the business. If you can't agree, *someone* must make a decision or the business will become paralyzed. Any scheme that works for conflict resolution is fine. Maybe you're the product expert and your partner is the sales expert, and you agree that each will make final decisions in each respective area; or you might agree that one of you will be the ultimate arbiter; or you will each fill that role on a rotating basis.

3. Minimize the number of partners you bring into the business. Often, first-time entrepreneurs seek to reduce the risk of the new venture by including multiple partners; there seems to be a false sense of security in numbers. However, each additional partner is another mouth to feed for your fledgling business. Resist the temptation to take them on board unless each is fully committed and brings needed skills to the table. This is not a bandwagon—it is a young and fragile business at its most vulnerable stage. Reducing the number of partners will also reduce the potential for intrapartner conflict later on.

4. Resolve issues quickly. If you can't resolve the issue and it's impeding the progress of the business, ask the partner to leave.

Chances are, if you have partners, you will have problems with at least one of them at some point. It's extremely important for you to have graceful exit strategies and well-defined, agreed-upon procedures long before the problem occurs.

Strategy #8: Just Jump In!

The harsh truth is, not until you're thrashing about in the heart of a new business that the hard realities really hit you. There comes a time when all of the forethought and planning have to stop, and you actually have to jump off the cliff.

Before going further, though, take a look at what Andrew Field of PrintingForLess.com considers to be his fourteen keys to success as a Bootstrapper:

1. Find a niche within a niche.
2. Choose a name that instantly means something to clients.
3. Provide exceptional customer service.
4. Big bucks are made in simplifying, not complicating a business process.
5. Use the press to broadcast your innovation.
6. Think counterintuitively.
7. Keep a hawkish eye on your receivables management.
8. Get customers to pay up front when possible.
9. Train your staff to be perfect handlers of customers.
10. Try to ride a trend, rather than create one yourself.
11. Don't offer drone jobs to great people.
12. Get everyone to think like the owner concerning expenses.
13. Maximize experimentation by embedding it in the company.
14. Keep a dog in the office—it's great for morale.

a bootstrapping exercise

Draft a single-page description of your proposed product or service. Now call or visit twenty prospective customers and ask them to buy it. Yes, really do it! After considering their responses, update your description and contact twenty more.

CHAPTER 2

MAKE SALES
JOB NUMBER ONE

"Nothing happens till somebody sells something."

—*Unknown*

A s an entrepreneur, you might have a great product or service that you have worked hard to develop. You might have hired a fantastic staff. You might have cash in the bank, a logo and letterhead, a beautiful office, computers on the desks, and all those things that come to mind when we picture a business. But that's not what makes a business. Only sales can do that.

This is good news for Bootstrappers. Bootstrappers can't afford fancy offices or large staffs, and they might not even have a finished product yet. That's fine, because Bootstrappers don't need those things to get started. As soon as you can start selling—that is, go out and find customers willing to buy your product or service—you have a business.

When you're Bootstrapping a business, don't worry about the nonessentials. Your first concern is sales. Everything else can

a bootstrapper's story:

The Art of the Pre-Sell

At RightNow Technologies—the company started by coauthor Greg Gianforte—there's a sign on the wall with the quote that this chapter began with: "Nothing happens until somebody sells something." In other words, sales is where your business begins. You don't have a business until you start selling.

In 1997, RightNow began as just an idea for a product. And the only thing that could make the product real was a sale. That year the Internet was just starting to boom. However, a lot of companies did not have a good way of responding to customer inquiries through their Web sites. Most of their software solutions seemed to be homegrown and rather ineffective. So Greg tried to imagine what kind of software could respond automatically to customer inquiries. One by one he made a list of features he thought would be central to the product. Then he hit the phones.

Greg called hundreds of companies and asked to speak to the customer support manager. He described the software and faxed them the specification—just one page, nothing more. Then he asked them whether they'd be willing to buy this product for their company's Web site if it were available.

A core minority said, yes, they would in principle like to buy such a product. Most companies of course said: "No thanks." But far from being despondent, Greg saw in this response a real business opportunity. When a potential customer declined, Greg went into fifth gear and started to listen real hard. The customer would be asked, "Why not, may I ask?" and then other core questions: What features do you really need? What additional features would it take to really make you buy this software?" Then the managers would tell him. Greg would then add the customer's required features to the specification list of his as yet nonexistent and entirely hypothetical product—and put that customer's name next to it.

Reactions to this "pre-sell the product" strategy yielded other instructive surprises. Some of the software's features that had seemed likely to be snapped up by managers aroused nothing but indifference. These were dropped from the specifications, an action that saved many hours of unnecessary and pointless development work. The beauty of the process was that it all yielded invaluable feedback. All of the favored features went into the product, and all the unpopular ones were discarded.

come later, and sometimes that even includes the product or service that you're selling. In fact, if you approach it the right way, sales is the best way to come up with a product that people will buy. Sales is the one and only way to tell whether or not you have something of value. The bottom-line message to all Bootstrappers is this: "You don't need a product—to sell it." The statement sounds extraordinary, contradictory, and even ridiculous. But it's far from untrue. For the Bootstrapper, it's the key way to find a product somebody wants to buy.

Pre-Selling Works for All Activities and Sectors

The principle of the pre-sell demonstrated in the previous story has the great advantage of being universally applicable. The tactic would work for thousands of Bootstrapped start-ups, low or high tech, across almost every sector and area of activity.

Take a home delivery service offering gourmet meals. If the mind-set of a traditional entrepreneur were applied, a person starting such a business would spend thousands of dollars buying or renting catering equipment. Then much more on chefs and catering staff, and then even more to ask focus groups to market-test the meals and see if the participants would buy them. Wrong move!

The home-meal Bootstrapper would do precisely the opposite. He or she doesn't cook a single meal or spend a dollar on kitchen equipment. Instead, the Bootstrapper compiles an interesting menu and then goes door-to-door around the neighborhood, into offices, factories, and homes, asking if anyone is interested. If the menu is sufficiently different, well presented, and affordable, the Bootstrapper has a chance of getting an order.

But, and this is equally important, if no one likes the offering, the Bootstrapper has not wasted a cent on making meals nobody wants. Instead, the Bootstrapper has learned not merely a useful lesson but a fundamental one: Rethink your product offering.

From your stream of sales calls, you will find consistent themes emerging—and this is the bedrock on which you will build a business. The theme might be a lack of good plumbers or difficulties in finding affordable garden maintenance or convenient off-hour meals. Make sure, of course, that you've uncovered a trend, not just a single example. There are thousands of undiscovered markets waiting to be tapped by Bootstrappers. All you need to do is to lift the phone and let people know you exist.

Many thousands of hardworking people start successful businesses through Bootstrapping, but all too few begin by giving absolute priority to sales. If they gave sales priority, a far greater number would discover the true potential of their venture much earlier in the process, rather than finding out through luck or painful disappointment.

Use Sales as Your Market Research

The practice of asking prospective customers to buy your early product gives you a true, laser-beam insight into what the market really wants. It's all the market research you really need, and the process is swift, direct, and often costs nothing more than the price of some phone calls. The act of talking to customers will teach you more about your existing and future markets than a dozen surveys or focus groups.

When this process is complete, you will be at the critical point in the Bootstrapping process—you will have a product that at least some customers like, and even admire, and, crucially, that some are willing to buy. You now have the beginnings of a business.

Not every start-up business is fortunate enough to create a product with broad appeal such as RightNow's customer-service

a bootstrapper's tale:

Find the Need, and Sell to It

Starting a business with nothing is exactly what Marcia Alcantra in Seattle did back in 1995. In an age when more and more companies outsource the actual production of the goods they sell to other manufacturers, Marcie Alcantra saw an opportunity in the print and packaging business. "The only way to make a lot of money, and make it quickly without risk and without inventory problems, is to offer a service," she believes. "The best part is that you don't have to buy anything until you have an order. So it doesn't cost you anything to do it. You find the need, and then you sell it. For me, the only way to get business is to have sales in advance and then go ahead and acquire what I need for that commitment."

Alcantra and her boyfriend, a sales rep in the printing industry, did exactly that. They floated the idea of starting a printing and packaging company. The pair had zero capital, a couple of leads, and a business card reading "Seattle Box Company" to launch the new enterprise.

After a month of wearying sales calls, Alcantra landed an order for corrugated boxes from a major seafood importer. Then, to fill the order, she found a supplier of boxes who could deliver the boxes at a price Alcantra needed.

The orders kept coming, and within a few months Alcantra picked up another account. It was very, very low margin, but it was very high volume. "I went to the vendors and was able to negotiate net thirty-day terms with them. My client was going to pay me in thirty days," she says. "So at that point I was off and running."

Remember, a Bootstrapper is not a conventional entrepreneur. You are not in the business of making a product and then trying to sell it. A Bootstrapper works in the opposite direction. First and foremost, the Bootstrapper is in the business of discovering a market need and only then making the product that meets that particular need.

software. But it's often surprising how the simplest business concept can expand, adapt, and somehow spontaneously mutate over the months and years to satisfy a mass of unforeseen business requirements. For RightNow, this high point was reached for little more than the cost of a phone bill—a few hundred dollars at most—and this example can easily be replicated by millions of latent Bootstrappers who want to start their own businesses, but are unsure how.

One important warning for a Bootstrapper developing a product: Don't promise to deliver the product immediately. At the beginning stages of RightNow Technologies, prospective customers were told that the product would be ready in sixty days. For most companies two months is a very reasonable period of time; many product cycles can take years. The first orders at Right-Now couldn't be fulfilled immediately, because there wasn't yet an actual product behind that spec sheet. But a product could certainly be delivered in the sixty days promised. In reality, customers are willing to wait awhile for a product or service, providing they believe it is worthwhile, and it is delivered more or less on time. In contrast, a conventionally trained entrepreneur would be in a state of shock at the idea of not delivering instantly on a customer request.

Give It Away for Free—To Your Advantage

In the early stages of RightNow Technologies, Greg decided not to charge all of the customers for the software. At the time, it was infinitely more important to get a stream of tough but honest feedback from prospective customers. Charging them nothing turned out to be the best way to achieve this goal. After learning what customers liked and didn't like about the product, Right-Now could fix it accordingly. A few weeks later, when the avalanche of tire-kicking, sharp criticism, and constructive (and, yes, destructive) comments had subsided, all of the feedback was sifted through, and RightNow began to incorporate all of the essential changes managers demanded.

Also, giving a product away for free can be less expensive than the costs associated with a longer sales cycle. In the software business, for example, where the incremental cost of goods is close to zero, the give-it-away exercise can cost almost nothing.

For the Bootstrapper, the ultimate goal is to get to a point where customers are paying you for your product, and often the shortest way of doing that is to "Give it away for free." Of course, the technique is not new, but it is curiously underused by budding entrepreneurs. A Porsche car dealer in Kansas City actually "gives away" cars. He's prone to asking a prospect out to lunch and arrives in a beautiful new Porsche. After lunch the dealer suggests his prospect drive the car back to the prospect's own office. "Would you like to keep it for a week?" the dealer asks. More often than not, once the week is over the prospect finds the $50,000 to keep the car permanently. Owners of pet shops also know that if they let a family take home a puppy for a week, the puppy is even less likely to be returned than is the Porsche.

Finding Reference Customers

Whenever a Bootstrapper is just starting out and he or she calls a new customer for the first time, the customer invariably asks this question: "Who else is using the product?" At the beginning the Bootstrapper has no customers, let alone any reference customers, so he or she is caught in a classic chicken-or-egg situation. The Bootstrapper at first feels foolish when confronted with the question.

But here lies your opportunity. If you've been giving away your first products on free trial, you likely have a number of contented customers willing to act as product references. The tactic solves the problem of finding reference clients, and again, it is all for free. Executed properly, this can be your masterstroke. Imagine you were starting a home meals business, for example. The Bootstrapper could offer to give away six free meals to customers willing to act as references for new, prospective customers. The process can benefit all participants—and in effect build your own self-generating sales engine.

Personalize Each and Every Sale

All customers love to feel they are getting special treatment, so if you can personalize your offering, you've got a far greater chance of closing a sale. At RightNow Technologies, when a potential customer shows a mild interest in the project, he or she is immediately offered a demonstration Web site that mimics the appearance and style of the customer's own Web site. After viewing a demonstration of a fully personalized, ready-to-go site, prospective customers were impressed.

To maintain the momentum of rising sales in the start-up phase, RightNow needed to set up a full production-line system that could churn out dozens of demo sites each week. Where could a source of cheap Web manpower be found? The answer quickly turned out to be students at nearby Montana State University. For $8 per hour, members of a loyal student workforce were soon hard at work creating Web sites for prospective customers. The level of loyalty and enthusiasm these sites engendered among customers was exceptional, and the effect on sales was electrifying.

Three Sales Obstacles You Need to Overcome

In the first few frenetic weeks of manning the phones, Bootstrappers will encounter three obstacles in the selling process. If you know these will hit you hard it is much easier to avoid getting disillusioned early in the game.

Obstacle #1: Objections from Customers

When your company offers a new product or service, it could be the very best in the world but this won't stop your prospects from expressing a flood of objections to it and dislikes for it. You'll be surprised and often shocked by the force and injustice of these objections. Anything that is new, that challenges old ways of doing things, is sure to meet with objections both reasonable and unfounded. No matter: Keep pushing ahead and demolish them politely one by one.

Obstacle #2: The Pain of Rejection

Rejection is never easy. But don't let early brush-offs get you down. If seven out of ten prospects quickly put the phone down on you, that's the average you should come to expect. In the end, getting a sale from only one or two of them is a great achievement. The world is full of entrepreneurs whose "brilliant ideas" came to nothing because the market simply did not exist. This is the cardinal error the Bootstrapper will never make. Don't be downcast. If you are rejected across the board, it is easy to think to oneself: "I know I'm right and that everyone else is wrong." Don't get caught in that way of thinking. See the rejection as a reality check. Change your product to meet a larger range of clients where necessary. Use their comments to your advantage. If no one buys, view the rejections as the market's kindest way of telling you your product idea needs more work, or that you need to rethink your whole strategy.

Obstacle #3: Enthusiasm That Doesn't Lead to Sales

Often a minority of customers show real interest in your product. Humanity likes to hear about new things. Your offering might be very new and therefore a novelty that is fun and interesting for others to hear about. If they are former colleagues of yours, they are likely to sound enthusiastic: "Come and see us," they say with a welcome in their voices. They might feel they ought to sound friendly, but don't be fooled. In most instances they have no intention of signing a purchase order. It's time to learn the lesson that you should not confuse enthusiasm with a willingness to pay. The three necessary ingredients for any sale are a true need, the required budget, and the authority to make the decision. Miss any one of these, and no sale.

A related problem to this is confusing shipping with selling. Just because you receive an order and fulfill it, don't consider it truly a sale until the customer accepts your product—and pays for it.

Making It Through the Tough Times

Prospecting is like going to the gym. The mental attrition is tough, and few can do it forever. It's not for the fainthearted. No matter what time interval you use to set goals for your sales team—monthly, quarterly, or annually—the sales performance "clock" always returns to zero. No matter how triumphant you might have been in Q1, you'll find that Q2 is a blank sheet of paper when April 1 arrives. The hours of sweat can burn out your staff (if you have one).

One way to ease the burden is to build a team spirit with lots of humor. If a sales rep comes off a long tough call, encourage the rep to repeat the ridiculous answers he or she heard, mimic the voices that he or she suffered, and laugh about the funny names that crop up. Promote comic relief all the time—it gets everyone through the day. If possible, pair up your sales reps into prospecting partnerships in the same way that police on patrol are bound together. Partners have a shoulder to cry on and a source of wisdom and enthusiasm.

Focus on Sales

To sum up, the Bootstrapper gains a far greater chance of survival in the vulnerable early months and years of starting a business by focusing all his or her efforts on sales. Some of the advantages are these:

1. You learn quickly whether your business idea is viable. No sales, no company—it's that simple. In the worst-case scenario, all you've lost is time, not money or credibility.

2. You get to talk to customers at the earliest possible opportunity. That salutary experience teaches you important lessons in how to deal with customers.

3. You soon learn who your likely customers will be. This information tells you how big or small your potential market is likely to be—and how much effort will be required to reach it.

4. You also learn what those customers really want, and how your product or service can be improved to meet those needs. Equally important, you learn what your customers don't want, so you don't waste time and energy building products that no one will buy.

If your product is ready for the market, you can enjoy some early financial success. You get some money flowing into your company, which for cash-hungry Bootstrappers might be the biggest benefit of all. Celebrate whenever possible, especially key milestones. When RightNow reached its first $1 million in revenues, the company gave a pair of boxer shorts to each staff member that said, "I feel like a million bucks."

Sales is the one job that has to be done well in building a business. There's no task more important. A lot of companies think sales is a necessary evil, but it's actually the lifeblood of the company. It's much better to have great sales and a good product than a great product and good sales. Realistically, both the sales and the product should be great. But given a choice, always take great sales.

a bootstrapping exercise

For the business you are running or planning to run, write down the absolute bare minimum of things you need to make a credible sales call. What could you do without that is usually considered "necessary"?

CHAPTER 3

THE NUTS AND BOLTS
OF SELLING

*"In the modern world of business, it is useless to be a
creative original thinker unless you can also sell what you create."*

—David M. Ogilvie

Selling is not something that comes easily to everyone, and over the years the profession has suffered a tarnished image. Many people have been the targets of slick, unethical sales reps who try to sell them the wrong financial policy, the expensive mortgage, or the unsuitable car, and they don't want to repeat the experience. Even for some Bootstrappers, the experience of selling might be an uncomfortable one. So let's get this tarnished image out of the way once and for all.

A Noble Profession (Yes, Really)

When sales is done properly, it can be the most noble of professions. Skeptical? Just think what life would be like without it. We would have to shut down not just the consumer world, but just about the entire economy. Life would return to the hardscrabble craft-based economy of medieval times. We would have to grow all of own food, make our own clothes, and create and maintain our own transport. Sales are the grease that makes the economy work. It is where "needs meet solutions." A salesperson satisfies people's needs. Unless the market is made aware of a better solution to a business need, the economy becomes ensnared in dinosaur solutions. That's why salespeople need to be heard.

Far from taking advantage of a client, a true salesperson spends time understanding the needs of a client. He or she might well deliver a product or process that could play a crucial role in increasing the client's revenues or cutting costs, and ultimately, delivering an awful lot of value. If you can save a company $100,000 a year, this is an achievement anyone could be proud of. It is also the ultimate service a salesperson, and especially a Bootstrapper, can deliver to a customer. If you achieve savings for your customers the last thing they'll think of you is that you're a "rip-off merchant." So again, banish this view here and now.

"Everyone is a salesman in their career," asserts RightNow's Brady Meltzer, "no matter what their career may be. A doctor needs patients, who commonly arrive via referral. No referrals means no patients for the doctor. Selling is no different to any other profession."

Salesmanship can be rewarding. "If one of your customers tells you that he got a promotion or a bonus or that he saved his company $1 million because he implemented your product successfully, that's personally satisfying," says Brady.

But Isn't Selling Nasty?

Not at all. But it can often be tough, emotionally draining work. That's why so many people avoid it. A day spent making sales calls can be exhausting, and for at least some of the time, disheartening. It has great highs followed by the deepest of lows, often in quick succession. This is the white-heat environment all Bootstrappers must live through, and live through it again and again. According to Don Springer, vice president of business process optimization at Webmethods Inc., in Boulder, Colorado, contact with a customer is the moment of truth. He says, "In fact, every conversation with a customer is a moment of truth. Otherwise you will never discover if you really have a business or not."

The Right Attitude Toward Selling

The justification for sales is straightforward. Companies are interested in buying from you if you can either cut their operating expenses or increase revenues. The true Bootstrapper must relate sales calls to the fulfillment of either or both of these goals. Once you understand how to relate your product or service to these goals, you are 80 to 90 percent of the way toward making a successful sale. But in both cases the key point is exactly the same—the salesperson must sell *and* ask for that order.

Ten Steps to Making That First Sale

In business, sales is truly the only job that absolutely must be done well. If you're a Bootstrapper who doesn't see herself as a natural salesperson, now is the time to learn the tactics and techniques required.

Step #1: Research Your Target Customer

There is a mass of free information out there in the age of the Web. Look at the target customer's own Web site and view the profile page. Read the press releases, which can often yield a great deal of the latest information. An annual report might be available for download, too.

Call the public affairs manager and ask any questions not answered on the Web site. Be open: Say you are interested in becoming a supplier. It's unlikely you'll do any harm, and you might well open doors you never expected.

Step #2: Truly Understand a Customer's Needs

The core of a salesperson's success is to understand a customer's needs, and then to address them effectively. Lon McGowan, iClick Technologies boss, recommends that you start by being inquisitive about the customer's business. On your first call, try to discover what the customer's Pain Points might be. Lon advises one should "engage the customer in a series of questions that opens up their real needs." "Let them answer their own questions," he says. What might you use my product for? Would you need customer service support? What price point were you considering? Sometimes use silence to tease out more information from the customer.

Ask open-ended questions—those that can't be answered by a simple "yes" or "no." Do not ask: "Do you have a need for my product?" Because the answer will always be "no."

Sometimes keeping quiet is the best policy in these initial conversations. "You can be more intimidating with silence," says Lon, "and you can let them run themselves into the ground—and run out of excuses for not doing business with you."

A young or inexperienced salesperson typically listens to a new customer on the phone, and trigger points explode in the salesperson's head as he or she starts to fit the product around the points the customer is making. But you must not do this. Nor must you follow in the path of young salespeople who arrive at a sales meeting and overwhelm the buyer with all the information in their heads. This way of selling has been described as "show up and throw up."

Instead, listen to the needs of the client—not just the complaints—and put these needs into their fullest context. Do not believe that your product is an exact fit for solving these complaints. What you can say is: "Based on what I understand your needs are, I think I might have something that addresses those needs." Then move on from there.

Take one example. A customer enters the showroom and tells a junior car sales executive that he needs a car with four-wheel drive. The salesperson then insists the customer view all the 4WDs on the lot. But the customer leaves. What he actually needed was a much more multipurpose and flexible vehicle—a combination of a people carrier and a pickup truck. Had the sales executive bothered to listen to the customer's needs in full—and in context—the need would have become clear. Don't just "hear one need"—listen, probe, and comprehend the true customer need. You will always be excited by the opportunity to make a sale, but you must take the time to listen empathetically.

Step #3: Find That Special Niche Need

Getting your first contract as a Bootstrapper is often an uphill struggle. But if you pursue the conversation carefully, you can identify a niche need that no one else has met. Say, for example, you've started a cleaning company. Start by asking a series of tactical questions: "Is the grout as clean as you'd like it to be?" Or, if you're offering an office meals service you can say: "Does the cafeteria stay open as late as you'd like?" The buyer might then tell you that evening workers have to send out for meals after 8 P.M. when the cafeteria closes.

The goal of this strategy is to increase the prospect's perception of a problem to a point where it becomes a priority. If, for example, one of the priority issues raised is staff turnover, you might offer ways of keeping up morale by offering meals to employees on late shifts. If you want the staff to come in early, offer to provide a breakfast service.

In the case of a cleaning service, you might first ask whether the prospect already has a contractor. The answer is usually "yes," so be prepared then to ask a series of gently probing questions about the level of satisfaction. Cleaning and maintenance contractors often do a good job—but they're rarely good at everything. This could be your opportunity. Emphasize that you are a specialist firm, not a standard contractor. The buyer might then state that "No one trims the trees in the parking lot. I've been asking them to do it for months." With all the many jobs required to keep a modern office block clean and well maintained there is bound to be a number of odd jobs you can do, and do well, for this customer. Undertaking a couple of jobs often opens the door to much more lucrative, longer-term contracts. Turn your edge into a wedge. Finding your "edge," or specialist niche, enables you to push a service "wedge" into the customer's firm and it can grow and grow.

Step #4: Find Your Key Differentiators

If you're starting a cleaning business, there might be hundreds of established cleaning firms in your city. To succeed you must make yourself stand out. Years ago Mark Hammerton of Wetton Ltd. started a business cleaning offices and schools, targeting both the private and public sectors. So how did he differentiate himself? Here are some techniques to follow:

1. Individualize your initial offer in order to get on the shortlist. Many big firms interview the three companies offering the lowest three prices. Instead of just sending a company brochure to the prospective client, Mark included digital photo prints of the customer's own premises in his submission. For most of Mark's prospects, this was the first time they had seen this technique. It went over well. First, this technique showed that he had visited the site in person, and second, it proves that he knew exactly what was required. This will give your estimate the feeling of credibility and personal commitment.

2. Be imaginative. Emphasize that you are offering the best value, rather than the cheapest price. The client will be paying more in order to supply a higher and more reliable level of service. One municipality, Mark heard on the grapevine, was tired of the high turnover of the cleaning staff of the previous contractor. Security staff could never know for sure if a new cleaner was really "their cleaner." They had to call the cleaning firm each time to confirm the new worker's IDs. This was irritating. Mark told the company that he'd be paying 70 cents above the minimum wage, and that by offering decent pay he would guarantee that most of the team who started with the contract would still be there in twelve months. "Spot the angle they like," Mark recommends. "It has often clinched a deal for me."

3. Convince potential clients that your ethos is similar to theirs, and that your service will be more personal than that of a large, anonymous corporation. Mark tells his potential clients: "You need to make only one call to get through to the boss of this firm. In a large organization it could be three or four. I think that will matter to you."

4. Play the "green" card. More and more organizations want to know you are implementing an environmentally sensitive, and even an environmentally advanced, solution. They want to be able to boast in their literature and to their shareholders that they are "doing their bit" for the environment. Mark foresaw this with a municipal contract when it came out for bids. His edge was to provide electric bikes for the cleaning staff for use on a large housing project. Municipal officers loved the idea. One even asked to have a ride on one.

5. Try the "technology" card. Some authorities like a systematic approach. Mark once brought in a set of wireless handheld computers for his supervisors. Each room had its own code, so the supervisors could go around the entire building checking on the state of cleanliness of every space after the cleaners had been there and reporting the status immediately via their new handheld computers. He was even able to print a snazzy report for the client. "Cleaning is cleaning," says Mark, "and differentiators are hard to find. Sometimes, as in this case, the quality of management and supervision was the differentiator."

6. Assure clients that you'll step in if something goes wrong. When one of Mark's teams let him down on a contract, he redecorated one of the rooms on site at no cost, and put fresh flowers in the reception and restrooms. The staff appreciated the thought, and the gesture rescued all of the old goodwill.

Marcus Bragg of RightNow Technologies remembers that RightNow's opening differentiator—being from Bozeman, Montana—surprised everybody. "You're calling from *where?*" astonished people would ask him on the phone. "Finding a uniqueness is not necessarily about what you're selling," he says. "If you're calling from somewhere distant, they're amazed and intrigued." Inevitably they would be delighted to get a call from such a remote and little-known spot as Bozeman, Montana. "They'd remember your call," he adds. It's a great opener for a RightNow sales rep. The rep can talk about the moose, the skiing, and mountains, and create a cozy feeling with the customer before the conversation turns to sales.

Step #5: Keep Your Message Simple, and Really Listen

The first rule of social conversation is this: Pick up on the last thing the person in front of you has said. In business, this can matter even more, because it tells the client you are really listening. Second, don't talk for more than three sentences before letting the other party take over. Use these rules during your sales calls, and do lots and lots of listening. When you've established that the buyer is listening, too, ask him or her: "What are your key corporate objectives this year?" Next, ask the buyer to pinpoint priority objectives in the department. What you are really asking is: "How do you get your biggest bonus?" So try to formulate in your head a positioning for your product or service in a way that will help the buyer meet those objectives— and win that all-important bonus.

Quietly force the customer to put all of his or her objections on the table, one by one. They could center on price, timing, or the weather. If there is no way of going forward, and a request to call back in a month's time is also declined, move on to the next prospect on your list. But before you do, leave your details with "Mr. No." You never know when that prospect might need you in an emergency.

If, during the sales call, you hear a concern, repeat it to the prospect. Then ask: "Would it be okay if I came in and gave you a quote on that job?" Your request for the order will yield a "yes" or "no" answer. In many cases the answer will be negative. But wait—don't hang up yet. Probe as far as you can and find out why. It could be that there's a business convention next week. Ask if you could call the following week. You should suggest something like this: "Can we meet your boss and schedule it today?"

Some of your prospects are keen to move forward. So first, find a starting point where you can do business. Remember, both sides are there to make money. Unless both sides make money out of the agreement there is no point to the discussion. But above all, keep your presentation as simple as possible. "The worst thing you can do now is to confuse people during a meeting," says Don Springer of WebMethods. "If you spend sixty minutes explaining it to a COO, he will then meet with his CEO—and need to explain in three minutes—a contract involving perhaps $500,000." You need to give the prospect a clear vision that he or she can repeat quickly and succinctly. What you should also avoid is a deep discussion about the technical aspects. "Many start-ups think they need to 'educate the market' about their technology," says Don. "No, it's too much detail—just talk about the business problem."

Step #6: Offer a Pilot Implementation

One of RightNow's best sales strategies was to offer a pilot implementation to a prospective customer. It was the classic "try before you buy" technique. Many would agree. Often, when the results are stunning, the sale goes ahead with little further discussion.

The ability to prove a return on investment (ROI)—in hard cash terms—is a big advantage. Because the pilot implementation proves that RightNow's software cuts the number of calls to customer support by up to 30 percent per day, the ROI is easy to calculate. And of course, once the software is operational inside a customer's business, it's difficult for the customer to find a reason to withdraw it.

RightNow salespeople sometimes don't even need to tell prospects how helpful the software has become during the trial period. For example, the firm's customer services manager might now be leaving the office at 5 P.M., not 8 P.M. That manager's bonus, based on customer satisfaction, is also rendered a certainty. All this because repetitive questions have been eliminated and customers are able to find the answers quickly themselves.

Once you understand how much value you're creating, you can persuade customers to pay some fraction of that amount. For example, you can ask for 10 to 50 percent of the savings you generate, depending on how concrete and how quickly you can create those savings. A 10 percent saving is often enough to get a customer to switch vendors.

Conducting a pilot implementation also means that Right-Now can move with exceptional speed. Whereas competitors often take twelve months to get their software into shape and to a customer as a complete solution, RightNow's pilot installations allow the client to see the system working in production in as little as a few days.

Even better, RightNow sales reps phone the company and walk users through all of the special features and functionality. The lesson for Bootstrappers is important: The little guy has as much opportunity to succeed as a big corporation.

Step #7: Ask Tough Questions

The Bootstrapper in sales mode must not fear nor fail to ask the hardest questions, even though doing so might "violate the social graces." These questions are the ones you fear most. Any one of them could break the deal you're hoping to clinch, and you'll realize that all your effort was in vain. Nevertheless, you will have to ask if there's a budget for your product. If there isn't, your efforts are futile. You'll also have to ask if your contact has the authority to sign a purchase order (PO) for your product, particularly for a PO of that value. If not, you must find a way of getting to the level where such POs are signed. But, in retrospect, you'll be glad you did. A tide of overoptimism can harm a young Bootstrapper's prospects. When the time has come to get serious with a prospect, don't hesitate to ask those tough questions.

Step #8: Now Ask for the Order

The moment of truth has arrived. Up to this point, your primary role has been that of a listener. Now you must bring the discussion to the stage where you can ask for the order. Asking for the order is the best form of market research. Only when you ask, "Could I have some money, please?" do you discover whether you are adding value. Getting a sale removes all doubt.

Step #9: Collect Your Order

Bingo. After all your hard work, let's assume you finally get the go-ahead from the customer. As soon as you get the green light, collect the necessary signatures or approvals from your customer. So what should you do next?

Step #10: Shut Up and Leave Immediately!

This is a must after you make the sale. Why? Because, after the sale is closed, the salesperson often launches into a stream of benefits that only serve to get the customer thinking about it all over again. And then the customer might even reconsider the order!

Sell It Once, and Now Sell It Forever

So you've sold your first product. Well done! But think carefully. Analyze how you did it. You've been through what is likely to have been an exhausting process, but you've now got an iron grip on the key features of your product that most fascinated your customer. This is crucial intelligence, because you can use that same information to sell the same item again and again, hundreds of times over.

All studies show that it's far easier to sell to an existing client than to a new one. For the Bootstrapper that means you are developing repeat clientele, which is vital to the success and growth of your business. Once a relationship is established with a client, consider that relationship to be ongoing. It's the beginning of a series of transactions in the future—your customer should buy more, and on a continuing basis. For RightNow Technologies, repeat customer revenue is central to its success. At one point some 60 percent of revenue was coming from existing customers. An average customer places more than four transactions with RightNow during the first two years of their relationship with the company and those subsequent orders increase sales per customer from around $100,000 to $400,000. That's how important repeat business can be.

Three Selling Pitfalls to Avoid

You might encounter a number of stumbling blocks in your initial sales program, particularly if you're new to selling. Here are three to look out for.

Pitfall #1: Don't "Negotiate with Yourself"

Often a Bootstrapper doesn't know the real or true value of his or her product, and as a result feels uncertain about its worth. "Don't pre-negotiate with yourself," says RightNow's Brady Meltzer. "You may not have a lot of confidence in your product yet. And as a result, you'll start to do yourself out of good deals." Work to understand the value you are delivering to your prospective customers, establish fair pricing, and then stick to your guns until you get your deal.

Pitfall #2: Look Out for a "Big Deal Hangover"

If you have just two sales reps and each one is concentrating heavily on closing one big deal each, all prospecting—the search for new customer leads—will likely grind to a halt because neither rep has time for anything else. Every ounce of your sales rep's time is absorbed in bagging the big elephant. This is a serious problem, and only strong management can rebuild some balance into the business. You should insist that "sacred" time is set aside for prospecting.

Suffering a "big deal hangover" means that your salespeople enjoy a brief moment of glory followed by an epoch of misery, because once the sale is bagged the salespeople have nothing left to work on. That's why prospecting should be a continual, ongoing process that never ends. You should be adding constantly to your deal pipeline. To build up a pipeline worth $500,000 might take six months. What happens when your salespeople stop prospecting? They fall far behind, and they almost certainly miss their sales quota that quarter. Worse, they need to do three times as much work to catch up, so it takes six months at least to recover. You might lose two full quarters' revenue as a result.

Pitfall #3: Never Oversell or Underdeliver in Sales

If your product is not right for the customer, but you've established a personal rapport during your deliberations, you can candidly suggest that your products are too new or unsuited to his or her needs.

Your customer might be surprised. But the act of admitting that your product doesn't yet address his or her business needs will store up goodwill for the future. The opposite is to force through an oversell and then underdeliver. In the end, you'll be left with a dissatisfied client—and one who is "unreferenceable." A wrong fit simply damages your reputation at a moment when honesty could make you an ally for the future.

a bootstrapping exercise

Define the three to five steps in your current or prospective selling process (for example: prospecting, identifying need, qualifying the prospect, presenting the proposal, and obtaining approval), the questions you should ask in each step, and the conditions necessary to pass from one step to the next.

CHAPTER 4

THERE IS *ALWAYS* ANOTHER WAY

"Problems cannot be solved by thinking within the
framework in which the problems were created."
—*Albert Einstein*

The Bootstrapper will inevitably come up against a stream of seemingly insurmountable problems. This is when the Unconventional Mind-set comes into play. Your motto on all these occasions must be: "There is *always* another way." In the Herculean task you are undertaking—starting a business from scratch—conventional wisdom doesn't apply. Your problems are unique, and it might take a unique set of solutions to overcome them. But remember, for every business problem there are many solutions. The biggest "problem" is simply that you haven't thought of a solution yet. But you will. You will always find a different way to move forward, and a way that doesn't involve spending lots of money. If the Bootstrapper makes a habit of demanding creative solutions from his or her staff—that is, discouraging the conventional mind-set—your company's fortunes can be transformed.

45

a bootstrapper's tale:

Hitting It Big in Las Vegas

When Mark Peltier left the U.S. military in 1977, he vowed never to work for anyone else—ever! Mark, by his own admission, was a singular and self-assured individual. But he is proof that one man can Bootstrap a business through his own efforts—and keep the lion's share of the ownership.

Mark was a skilled mechanic and craftsman, a more than competent designer, and most of all, he could work twenty hours a day. He had already spent much of his working life looking for that big opportunity. Living in St. Paul, Minnesota, Mark never found success with his earlier ideas because they were all considered "too ahead of their time." He was not a bankable commodity, let alone a creditworthy one. His early ventures were funded by a clutch of close friends, a faithful fan club that believed in his innovative ideas. He always paid them back, but never paid himself much money.

Mark was fascinated by indoor air-quality issues—not ordinary air-conditioning systems, but the real challenge of making indoor environments smell as good as the high-quality outdoor air we take for granted. With banks and other traditional forms of finance closed to him, Mark thought he found a unique solution to this problem, but a patent agent was another expense that he couldn't afford. Digging deep into his Bootstrapping instincts, Mark went to his local library and taught himself the intricacies of intellectual property. Within a few months he wrote and submitted his patent application. His idea? A device that fed microparticles of aroma through air-conditioning systems, bringing attractive smells into large buildings.

46

When the U.S. Patent Office duly granted Mark his patent, ten of his friends celebrated by giving him $10,000 each, and each got a percentage in his new company, Aromasys Inc. Life was tough, however. Mark worked on the prototype in his basement and he slept in his old car during trips to distant customer prospects.

Alone, and with no marketing budget, Mark wondered where he would go to sell his device. By coincidence, the leisure and construction boom was just beginning in Las Vegas. His idea was greeted with open arms. One of his customers, the Mirage Hotel, was overwhelmed with positive comments from guests raving about the pleasant scent of flowers, not realizing the scent came from the air-conditioning. With endorsements such as that, Mark's business grew until, by the late 1990s, almost every hotel and casino in the city had installed his units, including Caesar's Palace, MGM Grand, and the Venetian Resort.

Another problem emerged—if he wasn't careful, all of these hotels would end up smelling the same. So Mark taught himself the basics of aromatics, and worked to devise a signature aroma unique to each hotel.

Shortage of assets is no barrier to the rapid development of businesses. Such businesses must instead formulate inventive and highly imaginative solutions to what might at first seem like insurmountable problems. The stories of finding innovative ways of avoiding costs and getting over hurdles are legendary among true Bootstrappers.

The benefits are potentially huge. For one thing, you will be building a lively, challenging, and stimulating work environment for your staff, one in which creative and innovative thinking is the daily norm and not the exception. Make your workplace into the home of Good Ideas, and reward those who come up with true "strokes of genius" that accelerate your company's progress.

Where to find those novel solutions? Get your staff into one room and hash out ideas. It's surprising the quality of ideas your staff can come up if you put them in one room and ask the right questions. Ask them about their experiences; push them to think of ideas. Don't allow anyone to be laughed at; stop anyone who ridicules or mocks another's idea. Listen to all ideas, and choose the best ones. Such sessions build camaraderie among your staff.

Always Another Way

In the mind-set of the true Bootstrapper, there is no distinction between problem and opportunity. A generation of young Bootstrappers have found some imaginative and often entertaining solutions to all the obstacles they face. Here are some of the pieces of conventional wisdom that Bootstrappers constantly run up against, along with a few of the ingenious solutions they use to blow right past them.

Myth #1: "I need to use lawyers, accountants, and consultants."

In conventional start-up companies as much as 15 percent of the initial funds raised by the founders disappear within weeks into the pockets of lawyers, accountants, and intellectual property consultants. Sums totaling $250,000 are not uncommon.

For the Bootstrapper, for whom such figures exist only on another planet, an alternative must be found. Law firms charge full rates—but 80 to 90 percent of what they do is work undertaken by low-paid legal assistants. And the work they do is often filling out standard contracts on standard forms for standard clients such as you—but at "nonstandard" rates of $150 per hour, if you're lucky.

This is daylight robbery for the Bootstrapper. Instead, approach your colleagues, fellow entrepreneurs, friendly legal executives, and a whole host of enterprise and chamber of commerce organizations for help in obtaining these standard forms. "Shrink-wrapped" contracts and simple items such as nondisclosure agreements can also be found on the Internet.

There are plenty of ways to avoid the fees of predatory professional advisers. It's amazing what you can get when you ask, if you simply ask. Consultants, lawyers, and accountants can be costly and often add little value in return. An astute way of avoiding hefty professional fees is to invite your key contacts in these areas to join your advisory board. They will then provide you with almost free advice. It's easy to assume that because you are not a specialist you won't be able to understand the subject. But in most cases, straightforward business and taxation laws and regulations are not difficult to comprehend.

A Bootstrapper is often very capable and can grasp things quickly. The greatest thing about business is that, fundamentally, it is relatively simple. But this doesn't stop many hundreds of overpaid professionals from trying to convince you it's complex.

This is not surprising—it was members of their professions who added the complexity in the first place.

Every lawyer will tell you that contracts must cover all possible circumstances. But they forget one thing: There is no point in suing a Bootstrapped business because you don't have money to give anyone!

Myth #2: "I need a major new market."

In 1998 Sean Murphy started his company Optimus Inc. in Norcross, Georgia, to sell high-end refurbished computer equipment. His problem was one of fast growth. Dozens of customers were beating a path to his door in order to secure cut-price IT systems in perfect condition—but he couldn't fulfill the demand in such volumes. Optimus needed stock by the truckload. But where could he get it? What "Other Way" could he find? This was a true small business "brick wall." Sean urgently needed a gorilla-size partner, but assumed that no one would want to deal with him.

Then, two years later, a surprise opportunity emerged—in spectacular fashion. The fearless Mr. Murphy knocked on the door of Comdisco, then the largest independent computer leasing company in the world, and made an extraordinary proposal. He asked if he could resell Comdisco's entire inventory, which was costing $12 million a year to maintain in a fully staffed warehouse. "We offered to take it off their hands—for nothing," he says. "Of course we didn't think they'd ever agree!" But agree they did. Far from being a poor deal for Comdisco, it was in fact a total solution for them. The cost of the inventory was lifted from its shoulders, and the giant was rescued by a young and eager sales force with markets ready and waiting for this stock. "We had found that crucial partner who could help us leapfrog our growth," says Sean. Such strategies require patience. "Too many entrepreneurs make bad decisions because they can't be bothered to wait for the best solution," he notes. "We suffer from being part of the 'microwave generation.'"

Myth #4: "I need to use a marketing agency."

No you don't. What you really need is a group of satisfied and loyal customers to act as your cheerleading references. When you call new customers, you can immediately refer them to your existing client base. Think about it carefully. Does any one of your customers, let alone one of your prospective customers, give a fig about your company's "brand image?" Of course they don't, so why should you? All you need is a steady flow of new, satisfied customers.

Marketing was a challenge for Optimus. When Sandy Potter, vice president of business development, arrived at the company as employee No. 33, she was amazed. "They were turning over $80 million a year but were spending less than $15,000 on marketing!" she says.

Sandy believed in creating ideas that "drove business to us," rather than to an expensive and often ineffective direct marketing campaign. The firm spent its resources on a Web site and hired interns into work/experience programs to do all of the sales-lead generation. "They worked hard and found lists we had never thought of," she recalls. "The alternative would have been to use a telemarketing agency at a cost of $40 to $120 per hour per person."

Optimus goes one step further in its goal for zero-cost marketing. Much of its marketing budget is "co-op funding," which involves major vendors such as IBM giving Optimus $1 for every $1 Optimus spends on marketing IBM's products. "Often," says Sandy, "other resellers can't spend their co-opted budget—so we get their budget and are happy to spend it for them." This happened only after Sean and Sandy went out and asked if they could spend other company's allocations. "Asking" really works. Incredibly, Sandy's marketing department runs on zero cost, and shows a slight profit!

Myth #5: "I must order some glossy color brochures."

Must you? When the thought of producing literature came up at Optimus, alternative thinking came into play once more. "Today, all of our collateral material is sent out in PDF formats," says Sandy. "We are not going to spend good money on printing brochures that quickly end up in the trash." If hard copies are required for a specific event, they are printed on a color printer bought at a bankruptcy auction. Most of the time, however, materials are printed in black and white. "Nobody cares if it's color or not," says Sean. "The issue about the quality of brochures is a myth. Who needs all these fancy folders? Bootstrappers should avoid them. Half of our mail goes straight in the bin, while our letterhead is fully electronic." When a salesperson at Optimus hears the prospect ask for a brochure, the salesperson knows it's time to get off the phone. "Our top salesmen end the call quickly whenever they hear that excuse," says Sean.

Myth #6: "I need to travel far and wide."

In the early days, travel for staff at RightNow was neither affordable nor easy to achieve from Bozeman. Marcus Bragg, one of the company's sales chiefs, says that a few customers confronted him about this. They questioned: "Will you walk away from this business if you can't come visit?" He replied: "Oh yes, we will." It was better to spend the money on product development than on a plane trip. Again, Marcus found an alternative solution. Marcus invited clients to send their computer servers to RightNow's offices, where technicians could install the software and then return the servers. "Being in Bozeman became an Enforced Advantage," Marcus concludes.

Later, when sales meetings in faraway places became unavoidable, staff traveled on their own time over weekends to take advantage of cheap flights, and they stayed with friends whenever possible. "We did it to survive," says RightNow's head of product development, Mike Myer. "It was our ticket to stay in Bozeman. What a Bootstrapper needs is sales, not assets." He was correct: The company had the minimum possible tied up in assets. Susan Carstensen, one of the earliest employees, says: "All we have is people and plants!"

Myth #7: "I must partner up."

Should a Bootstrapper partner up? One of the mantras of the business world, and especially the IT and technologies world, is that companies must find friendly partners in order to survive. Partnering might help established companies, but the Bootstrapper should be careful. Such agreements can paralyze and cramp the real potential of a Bootstrap business.

Partnering often means delegating the sales process to third parties, such as distributors and resellers. Do they have your best interests at heart? Probably not. Rarely do such partnerships bear much fruit, and far too much time and effort is often spent on trying to make partnerships work in the early days when you should be courting customers.

It's better not to be at the whim of some third party who doesn't have your best interests at heart. Third parties such as distributors and resellers are often extremely passive promoters of your product. You might well be only one of thousands on their list, and probably one of the newest and least profitable from their point of view. Why should they bother?

Myth #8: "I need to buy brand new."

When Optimus Inc. urgently needed some engineering workstations, it balked at the $50,000 cost for new units. At a local auction, Sean Murphy managed to buy an entire lot—a whole room of office equipment, furniture, and even a microscope, as well as the precious workstations—for just $2,500. Optimus then

proceeded to sell off the items it didn't want for $8,000 to the los-
ing bidders!

Resisting the Pressures to Conform

Creative ways are not popular among conventional business executives. Unfortunately, the Bootstrapper might encounter a lot of
pressure to "be like others" among the same people you thought
would welcome innovation. These can include business angels,
venture capitalists, even your own bank manager. "Follow the
herd," they insist. In truth, they want you to fit into a stereotype
because they might already have invested in a conventional entrepreneurial model elsewhere.

This exposes an even deeper problem: Many entrepreneurs
make the mistake of trying too hard to be like others. The herd
mentality runs deep in humanity. But to copy or to follow others
is the very last thing a Bootstrapper must do. On the contrary, a
Bootstrapper's business must be distinct, different, and unique in
as many aspects as possible. This is not being different just "for
the sake of being different." Following the herd could be the Kiss
of Death.

Unfortunately the pressures are out there. Venture capital
firms frequently expect you, if not force you, to be "like others,"
because this is the only yardstick they know. If one company is
successful in one particular way, VCs expect all other companies
in that sector to follow the example—or else assume you can't
possibly be successful.

"Never copy another company's ideas," advises RightNow's
Susan Carstensen, "it's just ridiculous. VCs have come here and
told us that to succeed we should move to the West or East Coast,
the tradional technology centers. Their advice was wrong." If you
copy others, you will always be a follower, not a leader.

THERE IS *ALWAYS* ANOTHER WAY   55

Now Is Not the Time to Give Up

Sometimes a show of fierce fighting spirit is required if your company is facing extinction. Optimus faced a bitter lawsuit from the founders' previous employer, which alleged that Optimus poached its staff. Before the lawsuit was filed, Optimus was granted a line of bank credit, but when the legal writs arrived, the bank cut off the credit line immediately. At that stage, says Sean Murphy, the fighting spirit came out in the founders. "We sold houses, borrowed from relatives, and decided to sell our wedding rings if we had to." They refused to economize in the legal battle, and spent their cash on a brilliant if expensive lawyer. In legal battles, he says from experience, "You'll win if you bring a bigger dog to the fight." Their solution was innovative. Rather than roll on their backs, they decided to appear to their adversary as if they were on "too good a footing to settle." The suit dragged on and on, but Optimus showed no sign of weakening. The gamble paid off. Initially, the other company had demanded $5 to $10 million in compensation, but it eventually proposed to Optimus a much smaller settlement in exchange for an agreement not to hire anyone else for three years. Sean breathed a huge sigh of relief.

The Art of Barter

The exchange of goods or services between two parties, known as barter, can become an important method of getting key services for little cost. If you imagine that it's a suspect activity, utilized by rather dubious enterprises, think again. The German electronics giant Siemens, for example, has twelve people in Munich who spend all their time arranging payment for big ticket items such as $20 million telecom systems by taking payment in commodities such as oil or bauxite—or any other commodity it can pre-sell on international markets when payment in dollars is impossible.

a bootstrapper's tale
(continued):

Finding Another Way

For Mark Peltier's company, Aromasys Inc., a big break occurred when he met the Austrian-born cosmetics entrepreneur Horst Rechelbacher, founder of the natural products group Aveda. Horst loved Mark's concept and asked him to supply dozens of mini-units for installation in hair salons. The only problem was that Mark could not afford the design and development costs.

The Aveda founder wasn't discouraged. "I'll give you an $80,000 loan in advance, and you can sell them anywhere you like except in the hair and beauty salon sector." Mark agreed. With only three staff members, Aromasys now has annual sales of $1.5 million, and is growing 10 to 20 percent a year. "We could expand better if we mass-marketed," says Mark, "but we chose to be selective in order to avoid all of those demands for discounts."

Holding onto to his patent rights, Mark has expanded into the global market. He is currently busy installing a large Aromasys unit into Hong Kong's giant airport. The company has also opened a Dutch subsidiary to help sell his systems in European hotels. "It's a low attrition business," he says, smiling. "We rarely lose a customer. Other firms produce machines but we concentrate on filling large spaces very cost-effectively. No one can beat us on that niche."

Not only can Mark design, build, sell, and troubleshoot his units, he can do it alone, the ultimate in self-reliance. These are the features that make him such a formidable Bootstrapper. Mark said he was lucky to catch the Las Vegas boom. "We caught the wave," he says, "and it's ready to boom again. The good thing is that we're automatically a part of that growth. They're building a new $2 billion casino there—and we'll be inside it. No question. My next stop is to talk to the premium hotels in New York."

In the final analysis Mark is successful because of his ability to leap a series of hurdles, one by one, and come up with original and hard-fought solutions. He determinedly put into the practice the essential ethos: "There is *always* another way."

If you are a catering company, you can offer a dozen free meals in exchange for free advertising on a local radio station. If RightNow were starting today, it could offer to swap some of its software for free Internet connection services. You can also offer to give discounts on your product in exchange for a promise that the client will act as a reference point for half a dozen prospects, who might call the client in the future. Or, you might obtain the client's agreement to act as the subject of a press release, or to be profiled in a case study, or to speak at your forthcoming annual conference.

a bootstrapping exercise

Make a list of thirty ways you can promote your new product at no cost or next to nothing.

CHAPTER **5**

SCARCITY IS GOOD: THE ART OF THRIFT

"Necessity is the mother of invention."

—Plato

People have different reactions to those who are careful with their money. As a Bootstrapper you can expect a mixture of admiration, denigration, and even open contempt from those you encounter in business if you push, and push again, for price reductions, cost savings, and expense elimination. Ignore them all: Stay obsessive about costs and expenses. Saving cash is not a question of miserliness—it's purely a question of survival, of getting through to next month. It's deadly serious.

Whenever possible, keep an account of all the money you did not spend—and put it on your office notice board. Reward generously anyone on your staff who identifies and brings about a significant cost saving in the business. Show your staff how serious you are about thrift. Without doubt, one of the best ways of inculcating the spirit of economy into each new staff member is to emphasize the importance of saving money from the first day of employment.

When a rookie arrived at RightNow in the early days, the first thing he or she did was visit Costco, buy a new desk, chair, and the cheapest PC, and then come back to the office and assemble it all him- or herself. It was an important ritual that reminded employees of the need to conserve cash—at all costs. When RightNow moved offices, the staff moved the equipment themselves over the weekend. It saved $10,000, the price of using a moving company.

Jon Nordmark, founder of Colorado-based eBags.com, says this: "You need to practice 'Mind over Money.' You're frugal by necessity. You grow a better culture this way: Scarcity is good." Jon, for example, buys hotel rooms via cheap-deal Web sites, and he is always on the lookout for creative ways to accomplish tasks.

Now it's your turn. Bootstrappers' budgets face endless demands for expenditures on all sorts of "essential" items. But much of this is not essential at all. And finding clever ways of avoiding big-ticket expenditures is the mark of the dedicated Bootstrapper. If you can pay only 10 to 30 percent of the average market rate for a business expense you, too, are well on your way to becoming a Master of Thrift. Here are some more myths that can easily derail the unwary Bootstrapper.

Myth #1: "I need an office to impress my clients."

Start your business at home. All you need is a PC and a phone, a small workshop, or a garage, to get most businesses off the ground. Your first premises could even be dingy offices in an unfashionable part of town. It doesn't matter.

Grubby offices don't matter, says Andrew Field of Printing-ForLess.com. Businesses must make sure that cash is spent where it makes a difference. "Our printers are the best in class, and we'll put money into extending the functionality and quality of our Web site," he said, "but no customer is ever going to see my desk or my stained carpet. I'm not a banker!" His offices are housed in a former industrial building on a lonely side street. It still has a sign outside saying "Farmers Creamery." Staff density is high; only the boss has an office, but the place has a great atmosphere.

The truth is that much of the world's best creative work has taken place in embarrassingly down-market premises. This is best seen in the creative industries. In start-up advertising agencies, newly launched newspapers, magazines, and radio stations, the staff routinely share keyboards, the wallpaper is falling off the walls, tea, and coffee cups litter the kitchen, and the carpet smells faintly of something that happened there during the last Christmas party. But the atmosphere at such companies generates a superhuman collective effort that moves them quickly up the media food chain. Soon they become successful and the revenues flood in.

If one of these companies becomes obsessed with its own image, a great start-up can go wrong. It lives in danger of living on past laurels. Perhaps it moves into splendid new offices, complete with an executive dining room and a fountain out front. But, within a few years, it is near collapse. Why? Largely because everyone stopped trying. The old hunger, the founders' spirit of determination evaporated. Expenses are approved with few checks and balances. Most of the executives who founded the firm have left. The ones remaining moved into individual little offices, the politicking and infighting started, and worst of all, complacency took over. This cycle has happened so often it is a legend in the media industry. The saga is also a seminal lesson to any Bootstrapper who leaves the path of thrift. Maintain the thin thread of thrift for as long as you can. It is a thread that is easily broken.

Myth #2: "I need an expensive IT system."

RightNow's first IT network was built around eMachines, one of the cheapest computer brands on the market. But they couldn't be beaten on price. "We use open-source software for everything," says CFO Susan Carstensen. When it came to constructing the company's first database, the obvious choice was the Oracle system—but it cost $36,000. RightNow decided to use a simple open-source database system instead. This did the job just as well, and it saved hundreds of thousands of dollars over the years in licensing fees. Employees often believe they need top-notch equipment. They are eager to go out on a buying spree.

"You have to wave your hands a lot, and shout 'Stop,'" says Susan, "If anyone really needs something they have to prove it through performance first. Worse still, if one person has the latest equipment and another hasn't, it can open up all sorts of jealousies." Rob Irizarry, RightNow's customer services chief, agrees. He adds: "It's important to counter 'Staff Techno-lust'!" For most businesses, a cheap, basic PC and a fast, broadband Internet connection are better than a fast PC and a slow Web connection.

Your source for cheap, basic PCs could be mainstream businesses, which discard perfectly useful but outdated IT systems and phone systems (not to mention office furniture, carpets, and curtains) all the time. The utility rooms and corridors of even medium-size businesses are littered with the dark screens of PCs in nearly perfect condition. Many companies believe they have no use for outdated equipment, and the equipment has little commercial value. The nimble Bootstrapper should call up the IT managers of local businesses and see if you can take those PCs off their hands. Offer the companies little or nothing. You might be saving the companies the price of disposal, and they might be glad to see the last of the old PCs.

Myth #3: "I have to pay full price for the phone bills."

One big problem for small companies is their phone bills. In the first year in business Sean Murphy tried, most unsuccessfully, to get discounts for Optimus, especially since it makes lots of international calls. Frustrated, Sean went out and bought dozens of international calling cards and told his staff to use them. "I don't care if they have to dial 25 digits," he says firmly, "I'm not being held hostage by a phone company." Many small firms are embarrassed to ask for these savings, says Sean, but he tells his employees that "money in the bank is cash for your wages!"

Myth #4: "I need an expensive phone system."

When RightNow Technologies began to expand, its sales force increased in size rapidly. The company needed a new office phone system. But could it afford the $25,000 a twenty- to thirty-line system would cost? Absolutely not. Management decided to get a new business line for each new salesperson and assign each one an 800 toll-free number. But wasn't this a problem when customers wanted to be switched through to a colleague at Right-Now? Not really. The salesperson would say: "My colleague, and all of us at RightNow for that matter, has his own individual 800 number," making it seem as if this were a luxury laid on specially for customers, "and here is the number."

Later, when the company expanded to the extent that the 800 system wouldn't operate efficiently any more, an obsolete used phone system was purchased for just $3,000. A manager once complained about the system, which perhaps should have had been retired as a museum exhibit. The response he was given: "How good can dial tone get?!"

a bootstrapper's tale:

Something for Nothing (or Close to It)

If medals were handed out to Masters of Thrift, Sean Murphy would be a worthy winner. As one of the four cofounders of Optimus Solutions in Norcross, Georgia, he is renowned within his company—and now much further afield—as a genius for cutting waste and eliminating cost throughout the business.

Sean knows that there is much more to Bootstrapping than just thrift, but when he started the company he realized that preserving cash was essential. He was determined to derive every last cent of value from every dollar spent.

The company was founded in 1998 after Sean and his group had broken away from another company. Sean needed premises as quickly as possible. His search ended when he found a business hotel that had a conference center and office space complete with twelve desks, phones, and faxes. It was perfect as emergency accommodation. For a bargain rate of just $100 a day, they took over the facilities—but not before Sean had negotiated a free hotel room, including continental breakfast, as part of the deal.

Soon afterward, they found their own space but they had no furniture and no budget to buy any. So Sean's cofounder Mark Metz called his local priest. Could they please borrow tables and chairs from the church hall—on a Monday-through-Saturday basis? Amazed at the suggestion, the priest consented. "We took them back on Sunday," Sean said, "and picked them up again Monday morning!"

Optimus's printing facility was also Bootstrapped. Sean fixed up a single printer on a trolley, and the contraption became known as "Poor Man's Network." When a document was ready for print, said Sean, "you yelled out, found the printer, unplugged it from a colleague's PC, dragged it over, and plugged it into yours." It's never been particularly fashionable or cool to be a penny-pincher, but Sean doesn't care. He believes that Bootstrappers are a different class of entrepreneur. "Spend only where it matters," he urges. "Focus on the essentials to drive your business."

From the beginning Sean banned the use of recruitment agencies, relying instead on the "old-fashioned" ways of word of mouth and employee referrals. More than 15 percent of Optimus's current workforce was hired through employee referrals. When the founders had achieved some success, they went back to their universities to give presentations, and while there, met the audience afterward to seek out talented graduates for future employment. After hiring hundreds of entry-level employees and at least fifteen senior managers, Optimus has reaped enormous savings on recruitment fees. Optimus is now a 280-employee company.

Myth #5: "I need a salesperson but I can't afford one."

When RightNow started up in 1998, it urgently needed a second salesperson. Resources were scarce. How can you employ someone for nothing? Enter Marcus Bragg, the first employee at RightNow. Marcus was told that he couldn't be paid a salary, but he would be offered an aggressive commission rate to sell a product that is just right for the market. Was he willing to take a risk? Luckily, he was. Later, when the business gained momentum, the staff at RightNow was offered a mix of low pay along with handsome stock options.

At Optimus, Sean Murphy realized he had to attract top-quality salespeople, but he couldn't possibly afford their stellar salary rates. His solution was dramatic but effective. Rather than offering stock or big signing-on bonuses, he told the chosen candidates: "If you do business that makes $1 million gross profit, we'll lease you a Porsche 911 for one year." That move, he said, turned his sales force into partners, not staff. "It made our interests one and the same. It brought us on to the same side," he says. "Once they'd written the business, we could afford to lease the Porsches, and today we have seven Porsches and one Ferrari in the parking lot."

Myth #6: "I'm too small to ask for a discount."

Nonsense, says Sean Murphy. "Always ask for deep discounts," he says, even from the biggest suppliers. For example, Optimus is now one of FedEx's biggest customers in Georgia. But when Optimus started out, FedEx was reluctant to give it a discount because it hadn't built up any volume of business to justify it. Sean was not going to accept that. "Small firms feel they are not entitled to discounts," he said, "but that's not the right attitude. Always ask for discounts, and I mean deep discounts, ahead of your progress." Vendors will try to put you off, but you should insist. "Beat them up now, not in a year's time," should be your policy. Get vendors to tell you what kind of volume is required for a better price. That sets you a target. It could be much lower than you expected. The universal rule when shopping for services is to get three quotes.

a bootstrapping exercise

Create lists of the pros and cons to a business with a culture that values thrift, drawing on the examples in this chapter and your own experience.

CHAPTER 6

Managing That Precious Cash

"Cash is more important than your mother."

—An NYU business professor

C ash is to a business as fuel is to an automobile. No cash, no go. Although the Bootstrapper shuns more elaborate business planning in favor of just selling, it is absolutely essential that he or she does not run out of cash. Without cash, little is possible. Cash provides flexibility and maneuverability. Cash also provides the means to pursue aggressive and effective business tactics when they're uncovered. Guard your cash with your life. It is truly the lifeblood of any company.

Early on in the life of a business a Bootstrapper has precious little cash and the Bootstrapper needs special techniques to manage this essential and scarce resource. It's not simply a question of poor sales. Just as many businesses fail from too many orders as not enough orders. The reason? Poor cash management. Effective Bootstrappers need to perfect cash management.

In this chapter we discuss how a Bootstrapper manages this crucial lifeblood and also the purpose of various financial statements useful to a Bootstrapper.

Financial Statements

Everyone who has taken a business course is familiar with standard financial statements: the balance sheet, the income statement, and the cash flow statement. The problem with these standard financial statements is that they are like a rearview mirror on a car—they tell you where you've been, not where you're going. When starting a business, a true Bootstrapper has little use for these standard statements.

Without some way to look into the future, though, you really cannot operate with low cash levels. For example, you might believe you have a great cash balance because a check has just arrived in the mail. Then the next day a bill shows up and you feel that the sky had just collapsed on your business. In this section we describe standard financial statements and then describe a hybrid statement, called a cash flow forecast, that is particularly useful to the Bootstrapper.

The Balance Sheet

The balance sheet is a listing of all the company's assets and liabilities at a particular point in time. Assets include items such as your checking account balance, money that people owe you (account receivables), and any capital equipment you own. Capital equipment includes things such as personal computers, office equipment, and furniture—basically anything you bought that your accountant would not let you expense immediately and you must depreciate and write off over time. Liabilities include items such as bills you have not yet paid (account payables) and any debts you owe to people or the bank, both long-term and short-term debt.

Sample Balance Sheet

BALANCE SHEET—Marty's Cleaners	
ASSETS	**12/31/04**
CURRENT ASSETS:	
Cash and cash equivalents	$24,865
Accounts receivable	6,300
Prepaid and other current assets	2,262
Total current assets	**33,427**
Property, plant, and equipment	12,500
Less: Accumulated depreciation	(1,346)
Net property, plant, and equipment	11,154
Total assets	**$44,581**
LIABILITIES AND STOCKHOLDERS' DEFICIT	
CURRENT LIABILITIES:	
Current installment of long-term debt	$831
Accounts payable	4,200
Wages payable	5,560
Other current liabilities	2,445
Total current liabilities	**13,036**
Long-term debt, excluding current installments	10,101
Total liabilities	**$23,137**
STOCKHOLDERS' EQUITY:	
Paid-in capital	5,000
Accumulated profit	16,444
Total stockholders' equity	**21,444**
TOTAL BOOK VALUE	**$21,444**

The difference between the company's assets and the company's liabilities is the book value of the company. If the assets exceed the liabilities, the company has a positive book value, and if the assets are less than the liabilities, the company has a negative book value.

The balance sheet is a picture of the company's assets and liabilities on a specific date—for example, the last day of last year. This is the problem with a balance sheet: it is a snapshot and does not look forward. Early on in the life of a business, a Bootstrapper can forget about balance sheets.

The Income Statement

The income statement is slightly more useful to a Bootstrapper than the balance sheet in that it tells you more about your actual operations over a specific period of time. An income statement is also called a profit-and-loss statement, or just a P&L. An income statement consists of three sections: income, expenses, and profit or "the bottom line." Unlike a balance sheet, which reflects a specific date, an income statement reflects a specific period of time. For example, you might have an income statement showing income for last month, last quarter, or all of last year.

An income statement is very easy to understand. Various sources of income during the period are listed first and are followed by a listing of all expenses the business incurred during the same period. Both the income section and expense section are then subtotaled separately so you see total income and total expenses. Total expenses for the period are then subtracted from the total income for the period to give your net profit or the proverbial "bottom line"—aptly named, because it is on the bottom line of the income statement.

As companies become larger and more complicated, more categories are added to the income and expense sections of the income statement. However, even the income statement for the largest multinational conglomerate starts with this basic structure.

The income statement is useful in telling you whether or not your income exceeded your expenses, but, just like a balance sheet, it is a rearview mirror and not that useful to an early stage Bootstrapper.

Sample Income Statement

INCOME STATEMENT—Marty's Cleaners	
2004	
REVENUES:	
Cleaning Services	$86,655
Other	1,267
Total revenue	**87,922**
EXPENSES:	
Wages	63,000
Advertising and promotion	541
Supplies	7,234
Equipment depreciation	1,500
Restructure charges	–
Taxes	5,378
Interest expense	120
Total expenses	**77,773**
NET INCOME (LOSS)	**$10,149**

a bootstrapper's tale:

Striking Gold

When John Fanuzzi arrived in Montana from Philadelphia in 1980 with everything he owned in the back of a pickup, he knew his whole future depended on how carefully he could manage his cash. In the backseat were his two children, a five-year-old and a two-year-old. John was a single father. He was also an experienced construction project manager, and a skilled carpenter. And his business idea: to build a successful company from the unlikeliest of products—massage tables.

His Bootstrapping story began when he earlier suffered an injured back that doctors said could not be treated. But after one visit to a massage therapist, his pain disappeared. During that session the therapist said he was unable to find a decent, portable patient table for patients. "Oh, I'm a carpenter," said John casually. "I'll make you one."

With $100 spent on materials, mostly oak and foam, John created his first table in his driveway, much to the amusement of neighbors. His first customer was amazed. Then his friends got to hear of it, and orders came flooding in.

There was just one problem: How could John afford to lay out $100 for each table? He would be out of pocket in days. Answer: He asked for a deposit of $100, equivalent to materials and labor, and charged a healthy $185 per table. Cash-flow problem solved.

With no overhead, and with customers queuing up, John found himself working a second forty-hour week on top of his regular job in construction. After the move to Montana, he got local teenagers to assemble his products for piece-rate wages and shipped his tables on Greyhound buses. Once again, his cash flow was secure.

In the 1980s and '90s, the therapeutic benefits of massage began to be accepted by previously skeptical doctors, and John's business—which he named Golden Ratio Woodworks—in Emigrant, Montana, flourished. Soon he was doing $200,000 of business a year. Debts were near zero, and most customers paid within days, and in cash. The move to Montana also turned out to be unexpectedly beneficial. Californians and east coasters seemed happy to order massage tables from an address in Montana—it sounded "kinda folksy"—because they didn't want to buy from each other, said John. Their prejudice fed his market share.

Within a few short years he built a national business and was employing dozens of workers. A convinced Bootstrapper, John firmly believes that Bootstrapping skills, and in particular basic cash-flow techniques, apply not just to big businesses and hi-tech companies but to the smallest of businesses, even one-man craft businesses. And for John, this was only the beginning.

Sample Cash Flow Statement

2004 CASH FLOW STATEMENT—Marty's Cleaners

OPERATING ACTIVITIES:

Net earnings (loss)	$10,149

ADJUSTMENTS TO RECONCILE NET GAIN/LOSS TO NET CASH USED IN OPERATING ACTIVITIES:

Depreciation and amortization	1,500
Valuation of warrants/options for services issued	–

CHANGES IN OPERATING ASSETS AND LIABILITIES:

Accounts receivable	(723)
Prepaid expenses	564
Accounts payable	(291)
Other	68
Net cash provided by operating activities	11,267

INVESTING ACTIVITIES:

Purchases of property and equipment	(1,000)
Intangible asset additions	–
Proceeds from sale of assets	–
Net cash (used) provided by investing activities	(1,000)

FINANCING ACTIVITIES:

Proceeds/payments—long-term debt	(831)
Proceeds from issuance of preferred stock	–
Net cash (used) provided by financing activities	(831)
Net (decrease) increase in cash and cash equivalents	9,436
Cash and cash equivalents at beginning of period	15,429
Cash and cash equivalents at end of period	$24,865

A Cash Flow Statement

A cash flow statement is very similar to an income statement. It is a summary of actual cash received and spent during a specific period. The bottom line on a cash flow statement tells you if you consumed cash or accumulated cash during the period.

A cash flow statement gets closer to what a Bootstrapper wants to know, but, like the other statements, is strictly a historical view. Something more is needed, and here's why this is crucial. Without the ability to see into the future and project future cash balances, you run the risk of running out of cash. Unfortunately, none of the standard financial statements provide this most vital function of projecting the future. However, it's not hard to create such a statement. We will describe how in the following section.

The Bootstrapper's Cash Flow Forecast

The most important financial statement that a Bootstrapper needs is the cash flow forecast. A well-managed cash flow forecast ensures that your accountants will be happy with your balance sheet and your income statement. Let the accountants worry about those other statements—you worry about cash. The cash flow forecast tells you whether or not you have the fuel in the engine to continue moving forward, so you can do something about it before you run out of gas.

The big difference between the cash flow forecast and the other standard statements is that it provides a forward look at your operations and provides a framework for making decisions about when you can and cannot spend your precious cash. Rather than being a rearview mirror, the cash flow forecast operates like a telescope that allows you to see what's ahead.

In addition, using the cash flow forecast enhances your versatility and allows you to adjust your planning horizon as your business grows. More about this later. First, let's describe a cash flow forecast, and then walk you through the process of creating one for your business.

A cash flow forecast is a working document. To use it properly, you should update it at least weekly and probably daily as you make decisions on how to spend your all-important cash. Don't make the mistake of creating it and then placing it in a drawer, never to look at it again. Each time you make a decision about spending money, especially any recurring expenditures, you should update your cash flow forecast. Think of the forecast as the gas gauge on your car; if you went on a long trip without ever looking at your gas gauge, you wouldn't get too far before running out of gas.

A cash flow forecast consists of multiple columns, one for each measurement period. Each measurement period has a row listing the beginning cash during the period; a row adding the anticipated cash to be received during the period; a row subtracting the anticipated cash spending during the period; and, finally, a row with the period-ending cash balance. This ending cash balance then becomes the beginning cash for the next period and is transferred to the top of the next column to the right. Each column represents a period in time. For example, a period might be a week or a month. For columns prior to today, actual results are entered as cash inflows and outflows. For columns in the future, projected inflows and outflows are entered in the rows.

In this way it is easy to look at past columns and see if we are accumulating cash or burning cash. Also, it is very easy to look at future periods and see if we are projecting to grow cash or run out of money entirely.

To set up a cash flow forecast you do not need a fancy accounting system. It's very easy to do it on a sheet of paper, but even better to use a computer and a spreadsheet program because it's easier to make revisions and see the results of your planning assumptions.

Sample Cash Flow Forecast

CASH FLOW FORECAST—Marty's Cleaners					
Jan.	Feb.	Mar.	Apr.	May	June
BEGINNING CASH BALANCE					
$24,865	$24,732	$26,375	$27,960	$28,378	$30,847
CASH COLLECTED					
Cleaning services					
6,800	7,100	7,200	7,400	8,000	8,200
Other					
300	300	300	300	300	300
Total					
7,100	7,400	7,500	7,700	8,300	8,500
CASH SPENT					
Wages					
5,000	5,000	5,000	5,000	5,000	5,000
Advertising and promotion					
100	100	250	100	100	100
Supplies					
558	582	590	607	656	672
Taxes					
1,500	0	0	1,500	0	0
Debit service					
75	75	75	75	75	75
Total					
7,233	5,757	5,915	7,282	5,831	5,847
ENDING CASH BALANCE					
$24,732	$26,375	$27,960	$28,378	$30,847	$33,500

The first step is to decide on an appropriate planning horizon for your new business.

Your Planning Horizon

Your planning horizon is the period of time over which you project your use of cash. Some banks or venture capitalists ask for two-, three-, or even five-year projections. This is baloney. Trying to predict what your business will look like—down to the actual income, expenses, and profit years in advance—is like trying to predict the weather a year from now. It's worthwhile to have long-term goals, but spending days formulating detailed financial projections down to the last penny over faraway time periods is a waste of your time when you could be out selling instead.

For most Bootstrappers, an appropriate planning horizon is probably about six months, and in the early stages your planning horizon might even be as short as three months. Let's assume for our purposes that our planning horizon is six months.

The next step is to decide on the measurement period. The measurement period is the size of time slices into which we will divide our planning horizon. For our example, we will assume the measurement period is monthly during our six-month planning horizon. However, if you have a retail business, a restaurant, or any other business with high variable costs (costs that change based on usage), lots of transactions, or very tight cash flow you might want to shorten the measurement period to weekly.

Creating a Basic Cash Flow Forecast

Now, on your sheet of paper or on your computer spreadsheet, label six column headings across the top with the names of the six months in your forecast period. Down the left-hand side, label four rows as follows: "Beginning cash balance," "Cash collected,"

"Cash spent," and "Ending cash balance" (see Figure 6-4). Leave some space under "Cash collected" and "Cash spent" to enter more details later. In its basic layout, your cash flow forecast should resemble Figure 6-4, but you need to define your own subcategories under "Cash collected" and "Cash spent" to capture the specific needs and activities of the type of business you are in.

Now comes the hard part—filling it out. Predicting the future is always much harder than recording history.

First, next to "Beginning cash balance" under the first month, enter the amount of cash you had in your checking account at the beginning of that month. This is the amount of fuel in your gas tank at the beginning of this initial period. (We'll tell you how to get the beginning cash balances for the rest of the months later in this example.)

Next, under the label "Cash collected" list the various sources of money you might receive over the six-month planning horizon. In Figure 6-4, those categories are "Cleaning services" and "Other." If, for example, you are currently receiving some consulting income while developing your first product you might decide to enter "Consulting" and "Product sales" as subcategories under "Cash collected." If you have just a few large customers, you might want to list each of them as your subcategories. For example, you could enter each customer's name as a subcategory under "Cash collected."

Now, under the label "Cash spent" list the various categories of people and organizations you will have to pay over your planning horizon. For example, if you are planning on paying yourself anything during this period enter "My pay" and other categories like "Sales staff," "Supplies," "Telephone," "Advertising," "Loan payments," "New equipment," and "Rent."

As you use your cash flow forecast as a planning tool you will find yourself adding and deleting subcategories under both "Cash collected" and "Cash spent." This is to be expected and part of the flexibility of a cash flow forecast.

Once you create your subcategories, enter cash values for each subcategory in each column. The best advice here: Be conservative with your cash collection projections, and inflate your cash-spending projections. There always seems to be more expenses and less cash that you ever anticipate. So start by building this into your planning up front. Also, the further out you get, the less precise your estimates will be, but that's okay. You can make them more precise as you gain more operating knowledge about your new business.

Now, get a subtotal of the "Cash collected" and "Cash spent" for every month by adding the entries in each month column. Then calculate the "Ending cash balance" for the first month by subtracting the "Cash spent" subtotal for that month from the "Beginning cash balance" for that month, and adding the "Cash collected" subtotal for that month.

Next, carry the "Ending cash balance" from the first month to the "Beginning cash balance" in the second month, and calculate all the entries in the second month column through to "Ending cash balance." Carry forward the "Ending cash balance" from the second month to the third month and repeat the calculations, carrying forward the "Ending cash balance" to the next month until you complete the calculations for all the months.

Your cash flow forecast will show you how much cash you will finish the six-month period with. You want it to be positive. If it isn't, you will soon be out of business.

This cash flow forecast is now a working cash projection for your business. Update this forecast as you make decisions about how you will spend money and when you will collect money. If you ever have a negative "Ending cash balance," you must either cut back planned spending or increase the rate at which you collect cash.

The cash flow forecast is also an excellent "What If?" tool. Just make a copy and add proposed new spending plans to see what effect they have on your cash. If you have enough cash, go for it! But be absolutely sure that any expenditure you plan is absolutely essential and is the most cost-effective way of accelerating cash collected.

The Difference Between Invoices and Cash

One important point often overlooked by budding Bootstrappers is the difference between accounts receivables and cash. Just because you sell something in Month 2, doesn't mean you have the cash in Month 2. If you must provide extended payment terms to your customers, you must factor this into your cash flow forecast. One way to handle this is to add a list of sales closed, or proposed to be closed, below the "Ending cash balance" section and then project when the cash will actually be collected and carry the appropriate value to the "Cash collected" column of the month when payment is expected.

Be careful: Do not be overoptimistic—an invoice sent is *not* the same as cash in hand. If you must give "NET 30" terms, meaning the customer should pay you in 30 days, plan on at least 45 or 60 days before seeing any money.

More Advanced Cash-Planning Techniques

The cash flow forecast makes the basic business equation very clear—cash in minus cash spent equals cash left over. It's also an ideal tool to understand where the levers are in your business. There are only two levers you can push: get cash faster or spend less.

The first time you create a cash flow forecast and review the results you will probably be depressed. There's almost never enough cash to do everything you want to do. This is when reality arrives—a Bootstrapper *cannot* spend more cash than he or she receives. Period. You must either cut back spending or increase cash collection. Let's discuss how we do this. Remember, as mentioned before, to the Bootstrapper "there is always another way."

Get Cash Faster

Let's push the first lever and see if we can get cash faster. Many businesses assume that they must provide customers with payment terms. Even though this might be standard practice in your industry there's nothing wrong with negotiating different terms with your customers. For example, you might offer a slight discount, such as 2 percent, if the invoice is paid in five or ten days rather than the normal forty-five. Sometimes this is called "NET 30, 2% NET 10." If you can encourage and create incentives for customers to pay you faster, you will see a dramatic increase in cash flow.

Also, if your cost of goods is high you should try to negotiate a deal involving partial prepayment. For example, ask for 50 percent at contract signing and the remainder upon delivery. This might be enough to ensure you don't lose your shirt in ordering lots of parts or material to prepare an order. If you believe your customer might want to become a repeat customer, you could ask for payment in advance for a series of orders. For example, in our corporate cleaning-business example you could ask your customer: "Would you be willing to pay in advance for three months or six months of service in exchange for a discount?" Ideas like these are endless. Use your imagination; you will find ways to accelerate cash collection.

Spend Less

If we must, we'll push the second lever and spend less. Once you have your cash flow forecast created you should examine each and every item of expenditure—line by line—that consumes cash. Before you touch your cash, ask the following questions:

1. If I didn't have this item, would my business fail, or would it just reduce the amount of cash collected? If it's not life-saving, delete it.
2. If I need it, as defined by Question 1, can I defer the purchase for a period of time?
3. If I need it, is there any way the business can consume less of this item?
4. If I need it, is there any way we can buy the same item "used" at a substantial discount?
5. If I need it, is there any way we can barter our products or services for this item?
6. Finally, if I must buy it, can I defer payment in any way?

Put aside your ego and work out of your home for a while; buy the cheap computer until you can afford one with all the bells and whistles; pay payroll monthly instead of twice a month; switch to commission-based pay; buy equipment that will get you through the next year, not the next ten years; and hire students or interns. The essential idea: Challenge each and every expenditure of cash.

a bootstrapping exercise

Prepare a six-month cash flow forecast for your proposed business. Then use the six questions listed in the "Spend Less" section appearing earlier in this chapter to come up with twelve ways of reducing the cash spent during that period.

a bootstrapper's tale
(continued):

From Market to Market

Meanwhile, back in Montana, John Fanuzzi's business was going from strength to strength. His combination of design skills, carpentry expertise, and a keen eye for a new market opportunity—usually spied long before anyone else—was a potent mix. He started his business by making portable massage tables, which were hugely popular. In 1990 he visited a national hairdressing show in New York. "That was a zoo," John recalls. But he noticed that no one had a proper, comfortable chair where hair salon customers could have a massage as well. Back home he designed and built a model, and soon his massage chairs were selling coast-to-coast. But this clever move had far-reaching repercussions. "When we married hair salons with massage," he says, "we didn't know it, but we'd inadvertently created the day spa industry in the U.S." Today there are 1,500 therapeutic massage schools in the United States worth billions of dollars, and many of them use tables and chairs produced by Golden Ratio Woodworks.

Not content with that achievement, John concluded there was a gap in the market for a "wash and scrub" facility. So he created the first prototype for a "wet" table, where customers could be covered in mud, salt, wraps—or anything else they wanted. It was a far cry from anything anyone had seen. One of Disney's spas in Florida, and the Wyndham Anatolia in Dallas ordered them. Demand for his new design soared. "No spa, no five stars for your hotel," John told potential customers. Finally, Golden Ratio produced a range of high-end, all-in-one chairs that allowed customers to have a massage, pedicure, and facial, in a single seat.

John is proud that his company has played a pivotal role in turning massage from what was widely considered a "low-life" activity at worst and an "alternative" therapy at best, into an accepted therapeutic medium recommended by doctors. "They even have medical spas now," he says, "which was unthinkable twenty years ago."

Today, Golden Ratio employs seventy-eight people at a state-of-the-art facility in Emigrant, Montana—a symbol to one man's unceasing fixation with cash flow. Recently, when one of the biggest accounts in the sector demanded a large line of credit, John refused. He could not agree. What if that company went bust? His refusal cost him the account, but he believes he'll win it back. John knew that if that customer went under, it could destroy his own company.

John Fanuzzi's cash-flow strength over the years has also resulted in a handsome cash pile. Not content with starting one successful business in a lifetime, John has bought a quarry in Montana and is now researching ways to precast building materials from salt and rock as alternative cements in housing, furniture, and garden tables. A second Bootstrapped business beckons.

CHAPTER 7

GETTING PAID AND FINDING FINANCE AND CREDIT

"A sale is but a gift until it's paid for."

—*Sean Murphy*

G etting paid is an absolute priority for all Bootstrap businesses. Keeping on top of your accounts is vital. It's likely that hundreds of businesses a day in the United States are going under largely because they can't get their debtors to pay them on time. We know that over 60 percent of companies going into insolvency do so because of cash-flow problems. American businesses are owed more than $200 billion in outstanding invoices at any one point in time.

If you start out in business by sending out invoices on time with no delay, and offer discounts to those who pay quickly, you're on the right path. But don't hamstring your cash flow with poor debt collection. Too many companies fall into that trap.

Too few firms react quickly enough when they realize they have financial problems. For example, your bank might respond

a bootstrapper's tale:

Racing Against Time

Alasdair McLean-Foreman, an internationally ranked sprinter, started his sports gear business, HDO Sports Inc., from his dorm room at Harvard University in 2000. From day one, he Bootstrapped his business.

HDO stands for "Home Doctor Online," a Web site that at its inception sold home cholesterol-test kits. When that business failed to take off, Alasdair bought just five watches with heart-rate monitors from a supplier on thirty-day credit. He then sweated to sell them, and did so in four weeks. The next month he bought six, and he steadily increased his volume. His rapid turnaround was central to cash flow.

"Our worst moment was when we were getting lots of sales, but had no cash to pay the bills," he says. Without full payment of earlier orders, manufacturers often refused to ship new goods to HDO, which caused a delay and angered eager but waiting buyers on HDO's Web site. The customers often gave up and canceled their orders. On several occasions Alasdair took the shop's cash float to pay an irate but invaluable supplier—but always swore he'd never do it again. "'Crisis accounting' is what we call it," he adds. Alisdair's tale reveals how difficult it is to get your cash flow just right.

more readily if you give them some warning of a potential cash-flow problem. They will see that you are in control of the situation—and dealing with it. If you do need some extra cash, even the simplest finance package can take several weeks to execute. Your business might be gone by then.

If you're running a business, it is likely you'll be putting 100 percent of your energy into winning and retaining client business. But don't shortchange the importance of getting paid for all your efforts. Many small firms fear that companies will stop doing business with them if they take action against them for debts. Regardless, collecting money owed is what every company must face. Most public companies settle their debts in around forty-five days, although some government agencies take 120 days and more.

The Art of Receivables Management

The point of receivables management is to ensure you get payment on time—otherwise your business is in mortal jeopardy. Two months of poor payments and you are facing ruin. Andrew Field, of PrintingForLess.com, points out: "Receivables can kill a business. If you are selling $200,000 a month, and they pay you in forty-five days, you'll need $300,000 just to keep going." This concept comes as a surprise to many Bootstrappers. These are really big sums, and much larger than Bootstrappers often expect.

A Ten-Point Receivables Management Strategy

When Point B Solutions started in Seattle, its few consultant employees expected to be paid on the first of every month. However, Point B's clients paid at the end of the month—a thirty-day lag. The three founders knew it was utterly vital for their company to be paid on time, and to continue to be paid on time.

Darran Littlefield, the partner appointed to keep a close eye on receivables management (RM), says: "Nine out of ten companies have no concept of the importance of RM." Managers at Point B decided to put in place a strategy that ensures—as far as possible—that payments arrive on time. So far the policy has succeeded, and it's considered a model in the consultancy business. Darran adds: "We didn't want to take out a loan to cover our costs, and so far we've never had to." Such has been the effectiveness of their ten-point RM strategy. This is how it works.

Point #1: Establish a Relationship with the Accounts Payable Staff

Staff from Point B make appointments to meet the staff in accounts payable (AP) in person. "AP guys are often stuck in a back room—ignored and undervalued. They rarely have any contact with customers," says Darran. So a team from Point B Solutions pays a personal visit to them, talks to them, and finds out about the finer details of their AP systems. "With most companies their first interaction with AP is negative," Darran remarks. "They call up when there's a problem. We wanted ours to be a positive one. It is easy to fear an AP department, but it's nearly always unfounded." The move has served Point B extremely well since the company started. Most companies send off the invoice, kiss the envelope, and watch it disappear into a black hole for thirty days. They pray it gets past the internal auditors. Point B was determined to establish a relationship with their customers' accounts managers from the outset.

Point #2: Verify Information

During the visit, Point B staff makes sure that Point B Solutions is correctly set up on the client's IT payments system. "We checked that our name was spelled correctly, our phone number was right . . . that our tax ID was right, and that our rates were correct and accepted," says Darran.

Point #3: Get the Right Approvals

Next, Point B staff makes sure the sums charged on the invoices are signed off by executives with the appropriate level of approval for that amount. Darran advises: "Accounts are looking for reasons not to pay." After Point B began charging for larger volumes of work at increasingly higher costs to clients, it discovered it had to go two levels up the management chain to get payments authorized. Luckily, Point B's relationship building paid off. "AP managers would ring us personally and tell us they couldn't pay us without this approval," Darran recalls. "There would be a delay of two weeks." Forewarned, Point B could take action. Point B's knowledge of a client's payment processes is a real bonus, and close direct relationships with AP managers come in handy again and again. Weeks of anxious waiting—the fate of many a Bootstrapper—is avoided.

Point #4: Uncover the Nuances

Remember that all big companies have different AP processes and put their own nuances on the details. Get to understand them individually, advises Darran. "Find out the date they do their check runs," he says, "and get your invoices in there in good time." Send the invoice to the right address. It's no good sending the invoice to the head office if the accounts payables department is based elsewhere. If necessary, call AP to ask if they've received your invoice. Ask when the check will be sent out. "If they said they'd mailed the check on Thursday, we'd look in the mail on Saturday," says Darran. "Don't wait for the check 'til Monday."

Point #5: Look for Different Solutions

Check the finer details of exception processing, the rules AP departments use to handle odd items. Offer your clients 2 percent off the invoice if they pay you in ten days—that can be a lifesaver. Offer to "pre-bill" some of your invoices ahead of the next tax year, for example, so they can use up this year's remaining budget or increase your clients' expenses for tax planning.

Point #6: Try to Get Electronic Remittances Set Up with As Many Clients As Possible

This can shorten payment times by as much as fifteen days compared with paper-based processing. If you can't get automatic payment, make sure your payment terms are clearly stated as a condition of sale on your order acknowledgment form, and stress that your payment terms supersedes any buyer's terms. Second, on your account application form include a paragraph for the buyer to sign, agreeing to comply with your payment terms and conditions of sale. Show payment terms on all invoices and statements: "Payment to reach Bootstrapped, Inc. by 14th March, 200X." On statements, repeat the terms and show debts that are past their due dates.

Point #7: Make Sure Your *Own* Accounting House Is in Order

One day Darran, who was responsible for picking up checks from the company's mailbox, forgot to forward the checks to Tim Jenkins, a cofounder of the business. When Tim didn't get the checks, which he had always gotten in the past, they assumed some $500,000 worth of checks were missing. "We were ready to call the police on the suspicion that someone was committing fraud against us," says Darran, "when my memory suddenly woke up and I remembered my error."

Point #8: Be Understanding When Appropriate

In most cases, the AP department is not deliberately trying to withhold your cash—your payment is probably stuck somewhere in the system. It's easy to create bad feelings between you and your client's AP department if you hound them for money they've already paid you. It is up to the Bootstrapper to keep the keenest eye on prompt payment.

Point #9: Deal with Late Payment Excuses

Not all your clients are likely to be cooperative in keeping to their promised payment terms. If you're tired of hearing excuses from your debtors, make every effort to quash the excuses and move the process along. "The person who signs the checks is on vacation" is a common excuse near holiday and Christmas periods. Ask what provision was made for signing salary checks and paying utility bills. You might well find that signed checks were left to settle these important accounts. Put pressure on the accounts officer by stressing the importance of *your* account. Make the accounts officer feel that he or she is going against the boss's wishes by refusing to pay you. It might just work.

Point #10: Take Control of the Situation

Another common excuse is, "We're waiting for payment from one of our own customers before we can pay you." In this instance, ask the name and address of the debtor and the expected date of payment. Your client should be able to arrange some form of credit with its bank based on the security of the debt. Suggest your client do this and find out how quickly it can be done. Set strict deadlines for payment and ensure that all of your conversations and exchanges of correspondence are recorded properly.

Credit and Financing

After dealing with receivables management, a Bootstrapper should try to capture the attention of suppliers who will give the Bootstrapper favorable credit terms. On the basis of his initial credit record, Alasdair McLean-Foreman at HDO Sports was able to negotiate additional credit with more and more suppliers, and then extend the grace period from thirty to sixty days. As one supplier after another heard that Alasdair had been granted an extended payment deal by a rival supplier, Alasdair found that new suppliers would give him the thumbs-up on similar credit deals.

Getting Credit

If your business is beginning to expand, the gaining of credit terms can help release you from the grip of dwindling cash. There's no such thing as easy finance. Around half of all new small businesses get initial funding from credit cards. Bank loans are off-limits to most entrepreneurs unless the loans are secured on the business owners' homes. The best place to look for credit is often your suppliers. They want you to buy more from them and providing you credit might just be the best way for them to let you do exactly that. So where do you start?

1. Remember that getting credit is a step-by-step process. Start by asking a friend or family member who has an established business to vouch for you on your first reference application. Getting your first line of credit can take time and patience, but it's all worth it because it will open up the doors for credit in the future.

2. Provide a detailed business description that will "excite" the creditor. Aim to appear ambitious without seeming to be unnecessarily high risk. Initially, apply for a low amount for a limited period, with the expectation of working toward a substantial amount in the future.

3. Once you have your first line of credit, use it to the maximum. "Keep this first account in good standing and use it to gain references from your next suppliers," Alasdair says. "The first suppliers require at least two references in addition to your number-one family or friend reference. Always try to pay the first supplier early whenever you can, to sweeten the relationship."

4. Place a conservative first order and make sure you have an exit plan in time for the net-thirty-days deadline. If you do find yourself stuck with inventory, and all other solutions fail, consider posting items on auction sites such as eBay to ensure you generate a line of cash to run your business.

a bootstrapping exercise

Prepare a cash forecast (see Chapter 6) for your business. Consider what impact negotiating thirty- or sixty-day payment terms with your suppliers would have on the ending cash balance.

Do It Yourself (DIY)

ootstrapping, says Alasdair McLean-Foreman of HDO Sports, is a fundamental discipline. "It forces you to keep a low inventory, and to sell before you move ahead," he says. "You can have great ideas, but if they are unchecked by the limitations of reality, you're asking for trouble." He also refuses to cut prices. "Don't become a discount store, because you'll endanger your business by narrowing the margins."

But it was far from clear sailing. Cash-flow problems occur time and again. For Alasdair the key point about Bootstrapping is that it forces the entrepreneur to "do it himself." "If you DIY a business, it shows you how it's done—and unless you know how it's all done you'll have no real control over the business," he says. Alasdair produces all of his brochures and designs all of the Web site innovations, including the graphics, himself. To delegate this would take too much time, and it keeps him close to the core. "It is easy to stray away from the disciplines of cash flow, but margins in the early days are often the same if you're dealing with 10 or 100 watches," he says. "Bootstrapping is a self-correcting mechanism because it forces you to stick to the essentials."

CHAPTER 8

START SMALL; THINK BIG

"The longest journey starts with a single step."

—*Lao Tse*

Moving forward with a measured, step-by-step approach is vital if a canny Bootstrapper wants to keep expenditure within resources. You can't do everything at once, and you certainly can't do everything well all at once. You might keep it up for a few weeks, but exhaustion will quickly set in.

When it comes to your product or service, you can't have everything on day one. So take things cautiously. Don't attempt to boil the ocean. If your initial concept is so grandiose that you can't deliver, you're setting yourself up for failure. Taking the incremental approach means that your initial offering might be a "featurette," a component of a service that you can deliver today, with more tomorrow. Your first product will probably have limited capabilities. That's all right, because Bootstrapping is really all about incremental growth.

Call it "Incre-Mentality." If you're running a cleaning company, for example, your bigger competitors might just wash and dust, but won't clean grout, which takes effort and attention to detail. Many of your competitors might not clean carpets and windows because these tasks also involve a lot of hard work and a few broken fingernails. In both cases this is your opportunity to showcase your competitive edge by offering to perform all these tasks for your clients (at a reasonable rate, of course). If you do a good job, you might be asked to bid on other specialist jobs, ones that are often too small for the big cleaners. Because the larger cleaning companies don't want the small jobs, those companies won't see you as a threat, and won't try to squash you early on when you're getting established. In a few years time, however, they might wish they had.

Overall, far from being a risk-laden concept, the whole art of Bootstrapping a company is, in fact, a low-risk approach to business. The trick is to move your company forward only when the options are just right. Make a list of the top ten options—the most attractive potential business opportunities—open to your business, and choose three. Pursue these three until you find which one is the best opportunity—then go deep and hard in that one. It's like mining: You mine one vein of rock until the adjacent vein is better. But always, always, think to yourself "Who is the customer, and how much can that customer pay?" Given the paucity of a Bootstrapper's resources, it's essential you do everything you can to avoid overstretching yourself, especially early on. Move forward only when the opportunity is just right.

Timing Is Everything

Getting your strategy is one thing, but choosing exactly the right time to act upon it can be equally vital. Getting your timing right is one of the most common traits of the successful Bootstrapper. How do they do it? They stay current on what's happening in their chosen industry and with the customers themselves. Successful Bootstrappers make sure they are connecting a product or service with today's need, with an eye on what will sell tomorrow. An innovator creates a product for the future, an entrepreneur dreams of a product she thinks she can sell tomorrow, but a Bootstrapper builds a product she knows she can sell . . . today.

To answer the question of when to move forward with a new idea, Bootstrappers must continue to dialogue with their best clients, bounce around new ideas, and stay in touch with customer needs. This keeps Bootstrappers constantly in the forethoughts of their customers' minds. But more important, Bootstrappers can keep their fingers on the pulse of what customers want and see how receptive they are to new ideas. When the time is ripe and Bootstrappers see their customers liking their ideas, they can offer their customers the right of first refusal on the benefits and advantages of the new innovations. The move makes customers feel valued and can only serve to strengthen the Bootstrappers' ties with them.

Aim High and Stay the Course

A Bootstrapper should Think Big. Some business owners seem content with having created a company with a handful of employees that operates in a narrow territory. This is no small feat—but often a much bigger corporate entity with a nationwide customer base could have been created from the same venture. Don't forget: Some of the biggest companies were once Bootstrapped. If you aim high you need the stamina to build a long-term business, albeit with lots of essential short-term decisions. Conversely, however, while you should be as ambitious as possible in terms of selling your services, you shouldn't worry about hitting a "home run" every time at bat. Most baseball games are won with lots of singles and doubles; it is the same in growing a business. If you swing for the fences every time you are up to bat, you have a greater chance of striking out.

a bootstrapper's tale:

A Retail Store, One Step at a Time

In 1987 Scott Nash put down just $100 to start his retail business. He's a great example of a Bootstrapper who started small with a minimal investment, made sure he had a real market, and then built from there. Most entrepreneurs who want to open retail operations are forced to spend lots of cash on start-up expenses: renting space, ordering inventory, hiring employees, and so forth. Nash just started selling.

Nash was twenty-two and working part-time for an organic food wholesaler when a friend suggested that the two of them could earn some money making weekly home deliveries of organic produce. So they printed up flyers, passed them out, and acquired a handful of customers. Nash didn't own a car, just a bike, so they made deliveries in his partner's car; they used Nash's mother's garage as a warehouse.

After four months, Nash decided he'd rather go solo, so he bought out his partner for $1,400 and paid his sister $1,000 for a used station wagon he could use for deliveries. By its third year of operations, Nash's delivery business was bringing in revenues of about $200,000 per year.

By then, Nash knew that he wanted to take the next step and open a retail store. But he did it *gradually*. In 1990 he moved to new space that served three purposes: a retail store during the weekend, a warehouse for deliveries, and a mail-order operation during the week. Total revenues at that time were about $300,000 per year. Eventually Nash phased out the home delivery and mail-order side of the business and kept his store open seven days a week. Today Scott Nash owns three health food stores in the Washington, D.C., area, and his business, now called My Organic Market, grosses around $11 million annually.

Use Customers to Market-Test Your Innovations

Customers rarely identify innovations. Sorry, but that's largely true. But what they will tell you is their "pain points." Then it is up to the Bootstrapper to devise and deliver innovative solutions. Getting feedback is a vital tool in building a business into a bigger and stronger entity.

In product development, around 80 percent of what a company delivers is in response to customer requests. Seldom do the "Big Ideas"—the remaining 20 percent of truly innovative concepts that broaden the strategic reach of your product—emerge from customers. But they certainly will emerge from your close observation, tracking, and monitoring of customers—the hallmark of the Bootstrapper who takes a close interest in his or her market.

The focused Bootstrapper will reach for the nearest low-hanging fruit that he or she can next identify. Let's take a look again at our meal delivery service example we've talked about in earlier chapters. If the delivery service supplies evening meals for nurses, the Bootstrapper could go into breakfast catering. If the business started out delivering meals to hospital workers, the Bootstrapper could move onto nursing homes. Or he or she could add ten new meal options for existing customers. The Bootstrapper can expand into a new sector or expand the product line—or both! The opportunities for reformatting the initial concept are infinite. If you run out of ideas, revisit your most loyal customers. Talking with them is sure to give you the first inklings of new ideas.

The best way to develop a Bootstrapped company is to allow experimentation—but make sure the cost of the experiments doesn't "bet the farm." In 2002, RightNow put together what the company thought would be a real winner with customers:

a wireless-connected PDA device that linked customers with their RightNow database. At a user conference in Montana, with 350 customers in the room, a mock-up of the innovation was proudly unveiled. At the end, the RightNow presenters asked that any customers interested in pursuing the innovation come up to the podium afterward. No one came forward. Thankfully, the mock-up had taken minimal resources to build. The project was shelved.

RightNow's experience serves as a lesson: If customers don't see a need for a new idea, the Bootstrapper must drop it immediately and find something that does meet customer needs. There's a lesson in humility here, too. Too many entrepreneurs see themselves as individuals whose opinions are superior and therefore overwhelmingly correct. The Bootstrapper knows better. No matter how clever or how useful you believe your innovation might be, if your customer disagrees, it's all over. In fact, your opinion doesn't matter. It's not even relevant. Your gizmo might well have solved, cheaply and easily, a lot of your customers' problems at a stroke. That's not the point. For the Bootstrapper there is absolutely no point in being right and poor.

Changing Direction to Save the Company

In many instances your first product or service will be a partial success at best. Changing tack—moving to a different product sector or completely redesigning your offering—might be essential to save the business. But fear not. Most companies undergo radical transformations, and a great many undertake five or more changes of direction. It's quite normal.

Lon McGowan of iClick Technologies in Seattle assumed that the retail sector would be a "natural fit" for his digital cameras. Weeks went by as he tried to interest retail stores in the cameras. Weeks turned into months. No one would bite. He found out that the selling effort required in the retail sector was enormous, and the margins too small. "Partnering with retail wouldn't have worked without much greater resources," he says. Then, with his cash flow at a critical low point, the right sector emerged in the most unexpected of markets. It was the Give Away market, in this case the one in which major firms give away free cameras as part of their major promotions. "It was a development no one had predicted," says Lon. "The easiest way of distributing products isn't always the best." In this market niche iClick could be singled out as a major force, against a background of much larger competition, as a premium supplier of cameras and MP3 players in the Give Away market.

Learning to Say "No!"

In developing your business, don't underestimate the value of your product if you have a good one. Be prepared to walk away if customers won't pay for it. It's much better to be involved in a high-margin, small-volume business than the reverse. Entrepreneurs are often scared of asking for that higher tariff. At one point, Tim Jenkins of Point B Solutions says: "We thought: No, we're good. We'll charge them more and we won't feel embarrassed." One big firm, a steady repeat customer of Point B, was centrally managed with an aggressive cost-cutting policy and a procurement department that was bureaucratic and slow. Bitter arguments with the procurement department over price went unresolved. In the end, Point B refused to cut prices—point blank.

"They had divorced the business function from their cash policy, and we weren't going to suffer for that," says Tim. "It was hard to walk away but we simply weren't willing to cut our prices. And nor should any Bootstrapper." At the first sign of distress, many companies cut their prices. That's a slippery slope. If your competitors cut their prices they're eroding their margins and becoming a weaker business. "If you cut once," Tim adds, "all of your clients will want the price cut, and then more price cuts."

Never Delegate the Initial Sales Process to Others

Sales is the primary duty of the Bootstrapper, and as we've said at the outset, it must be the most important focus in your business. Sales is a job that Bootstrappers cannot and must not delegate completely, even after the business is off the ground. The Bootstrapper makes commitments—personal commitments—in the early phase, and the integrity of the business relies upon his or her word. In the early stages of the business, there is really only one person who can and should be handling sales. That person is you, the Bootstrapper. This you cannot pass on to others. Why? Because until the entrepreneur has worked out precisely the steps needed to successfully sell the company's goods, he or she cannot pass on that knowledge and skills to the first few salespeople hired.

If the Bootstrapper is not a salesperson, and not the best salesperson in the business, then he or she is nothing. After the first few sales successes, an entrepreneur who is not a Bootstrapper often decides to take a backseat and become distanced from firsthand experience. In distancing from the customer, the entrepreneur loses touch with customers and loses out on gaining valuable feedback. If this occurs, the entrepreneur has simply become the company's first, and most bloated, overhead item.

A Leader Leads by Example

It is the duty of a Bootstrapper to be able to sell the product, and this ability forms an important element in his or her future leadership. If the sales force knows the boss can't sell, it won't have any respect for the boss and even less for the product. But if the boss can sell, there's no excuse for underperformance by anyone on the sales team. "If I can make my quota, so can you," was the message, says Mike Myer, RightNow's head of product development. "Every dollar we made went toward hiring more sales staff." Selling became the mantra of the company. Nothing else mattered as much, he recalls. If a rep's sales target was $50,000 a month, and that target was met, RightNow would go out and hire two more salespeople. And so the sales force grew rapidly.

The pressure to perform was considerable, so it was important to have the right people on the team. RightNow knew the dangers of having one person onboard who wasn't happy and wasn't performing. "If you're a ten-man crew," says Mike, "a bad apple is worse than an empty seat." The unhappiness of one can impact the productivity of others. If you imagine the productivity loss of discontented salespeople is something like 10 percent, it's more like 30 percent! When a salesperson is not happy, a Bootstrapper has no alternative but to act swiftly. Give him or her one last chance—a thirty-day performance improvement plan. If the quota is still unmet, ask the salesperson to pack up and leave immediately. "It's a case of 'okay or out,'" says Mike.

Pick an Advisory Board

One particularly effective way of boosting your business is to assemble an informal, unpaid advisory board of experienced businesspeople whom you like and trust. Andy Mulholland, chief technology officer for the management consultants Capgemini, says: "Over time they are likely to provide you with solid assistance—at very little cost." Increasingly, American start-ups are offering seats on their advisory boards to their future key customers, an interesting development. Early adopters—those who always want the latest technology—or even established technology companies

a bootstrapper's tale:

Coping in a Crisis

Inevitably your business will be faced with various crises along the way. If you can survive your first crisis, statistics show your company will probably survive in the long term. If you can foresee these crises early on, often by keeping a keen eye on your cash flow, you have sufficient time to take action. Jon Nordmark faced such a crisis at his online luggage firm eBags.com after the collapse in the luggage market following 9/11. He came close to disaster but fought his way back to profitability in an environment where many others did not survive.

In the aftermath of 9/11, retail luggage sales went flat and 25 percent of Jon's workforce had to be laid off. Many employees had dedicated themselves to the business. "It was hugely deflating," says Jon. "We'd built a very family-oriented atmosphere in the start-up phase and we'd all got very close." But by then the business was losing $1.5 million a month. "Every day, cash was just gushing out," Jon recalls. "At that time no one knew how to make money on the Internet. Our business was on a knife edge."

How could eBags be saved? As it goes in many new businesses, Jon's first products launched the company but couldn't sustain it, so he was forced to search for a longer-term solution. First, with conventional travel luggage sales at rock bottom, eBags.com began to focus on other product areas, such as business cases, school backpacks, and handbags. "We found new opportunities in what we'd regarded as peripheral areas," Jon notes. "Handbags grew at a rate of 100 percent a year, year on year." It was survival all right. In the aftermath of 9/11, more than 500 specialty luggage stores went out of business in the United States. "Hardship helps you find out if you are resilient," Jon says.

108

But for eBags, new products were only one part of the answer. In a crisis meeting, Jon asked everyone to contribute ideas. One farsighted colleague said: "We need to focus on three things, and only on these three." As a result, one group of staff members was put to work on the problem of gaining more Web site traffic, a second group was assigned to improving sales conversion rates, and a third group concentrated on ways to increase the company's database of customers through e-mail. "At this time," says Jon, "nobody knew how to make money out of the Internet." But what he introduced was absolute clarity and simplicity into the process of recalibrating the business. "We introduced 'Single Issue Thinking.' We did everything to make it less complex," he adds. "People knew precisely what they were going to do every day when they came into work."

Slowly but surely, the three work groups made steady progress and the results began to swing round. Equally important, says Jon, they stayed focused on eBags' luggage niche. "We didn't try to grow faster than the market would let us. Don't forget: People adopt things slowly." Jon kept going, and by 2002 his firm became profitable. eBags.com sold one million bags in 2003—the equivalent to the sales of seventy specialty luggage stores, and a third of the three million items sold by Samsonite each year. Most recently, eBags started a site named Shoedini.com, to help the many thousands of customers who want to buy handbags and shoes together as one package. It has been an instant success. Jon Nordmark also saw that female customers want to buy a handbag to match a business briefcase, for example. These "double purchase" orders are invaluable, and increase the overall frequency of visitors who visited the Web site.

who might complement your product in the short term, would be examples of some of the best people you should have on your advisory board. In short, an advisory board can establish win-win relationships for all concerned.

a bootstrapping exercise

Which of the "Bootstrapper's Tales" in this book so far best matches the business you are running or plan on starting? What lessons from that person's experience can you apply to your own business?

CHAPTER **9**

MARKETING ON
A SHOESTRING

"Ideas and products and messages and
behaviors spread just like viruses do."
—*Malcolm Gladwell*

M arketing is not a euphemism for sales. Marketing's
primary role is to engage in activities that make sales
more efficient and shorten the sales cycle. In reality,
building a business is like waging war. In war "you either make
bullets or you shoot them." Every other activity plays a support-
ing role to those two functions, without exception. In business,
building a product or service is the equivalent of making bullets
in war. Also, selling is the equivalent of shooting bullets in war.
Every other task in business supports either building the product
or service or selling it.

If sales uses the "rifle approach," marketing adopts the shot-
gun. Marketing should generate the leads that are put in front of
the sales force. In the best Bootstrapped companies, marketing
is always subordinate to sales. (At this level, brand image, which

111

is a big concern for large companies and a focus of many market-ing campaigns, is irrelevant to the Bootstrapper.) For many Boot-strappers, mainstream marketing is of minor importance, but some carefully focused and planned marketing can really help your business. Once again, as with all Bootstrapping activities, your goal is to execute the marketing plan for as little outlay as possible. When comparing the various marketing options open to you, the first question is: What is the cost to generate each quali-fied lead? The second question is: How can I source 100 to 200 superior leads with the marketing options available to me?

Conventional Market Research— Is It Really Worth It?

Traditional entrepreneurship courses teach that you must engage in comprehensive market research. Here are five hard reasons why the Bootstrapper should steer clear of this:

1. **Market research is costly.** The cost is often way beyond the budget of most Bootstrappers.

2. **Market research, by its nature, is very indirect.** It is therefore contrary to the Bootstrapper's essential need to get close to customers. It can only add distance and a series of human bar-riers and unreliable filters between the Bootstrapper and custom-ers, which is the very last thing the Bootstrapper wants to occur.

3. **Market research is time-consuming.** The Bootstrap-per has only a limited time to launch a successful business, so waiting six to eight weeks for a research report is risking failure.

4. **Market research is often ineffective.** Focus groups measure only enthusiasm, not true willingness to buy.

5. **Most important, market research is notoriously inac-curate.** Rarely do market researchers uncover innovative ideas, which are precisely what the Bootstrapper is looking for most.

The flaw in market research is simple. Why organize a focus group to ask prospective customers if they would buy a product, when you could just as easily go ask them yourself, and build those all-important, one-to-one business relationships at the same time? A Bootstrapper who is awash in start-up capital can hire a marketing firm to run a series of focus groups and undertake surveys of potential customers to figure out what the market wants. But the other way—contacting prospects yourself—doesn't cost anything. And when you are finished, you might already have a stack of orders. If you don't, and if no one wants to buy your product, you will have learned quickly and relatively painlessly that you didn't have a viable business idea.

To Advertise or Not to Advertise?

The answer is, don't advertise. There's a widespread view that advertising is far less effective now than it was twenty years ago. Today, it seems that only a long series of appearances in ads has any effect. Advertising is useful only to big companies that have little to differentiate themselves from competitors. It is not a powerful business tool for small companies. Also, advertising rarely creates new markets—the one overriding requirement of the Bootstrapper. It is really for mature markets only, when all other new avenues have been exhausted. For the Bootstrapper, advertising is invariably far too expensive and difficult to justify in terms of results.

How to Be an Effective Marketer

For some Bootstrappers, like Paul Szydlowski of Prime Valet Cleaners, marketing is important. After fourteen years on the front line, Paul identified the various methods that worked for him during the ups and downs of his dry cleaning business. Here's how Paul achieved his goals through marketing.

The Thirteen Top Rules of Marketing

Rule #1: Pick One Message

By selecting one message, you provide limitless simplicity in the mind of the consumer. "Simplicity is no simple thing," Charlie Chaplin once said. But Paul insists: "Make this message something you can repeat over and over again." So many firms have muddy, unclear approaches that it's difficult for the ordinary customer to remember them. Paul concentrated in the early days on the novelty of the pickup and delivery of dry cleaning. In the early 1990s, you could get pizza delivered, but not dry cleaning. Paul set out to tell the world that this was exactly what he did.

If you put your one message into a single, but singularly memorable phrase, you've got a great marketing tool. It could be the name of your company, for example. Andrew Field transformed his business into a global player when he changed the name of his printing business to "PrintingForLess.com." Everyone remembered it; everyone also understood what it meant.

Rule #2: Pick a Consistent, Clear Message

Why? Because consistency and clarity help customers remember your product. Paul chose a photo of an attractive woman in a white gown as his logo. It soon became his firm's signature image. Across the breadth of his literature, packaging, handouts, advertising, and banners, everyone saw this same image consistently and came to identify it with Prime Valet.

Marketing for a Bootstrapper is also about creating maximum clarity on what your products offer. On the eBags.com site, the photos, captions, and customer testimonials are all aimed at giving the customer the clearest and most accurate description of the goods. "We want them to know precisely what they are getting," says Jon Nordmark. "We put the most realistic pictures of the product on the site." Lon McGowan, boss of iClick, agrees.

For his company, the issue of design is in providing a crystal-clear visual offering. He realized early that the packaging of his cameras provided essential appeal to customers. Cool design was key. So important was design that Lon appointed a full-time in-house designer as his third employee. iClick now has a full photo studio on site—all for the cost of $1,000. "We produce far better product photos than our competitors', which often look awful," Lon says. The iClick HQ in Seattle—a sizable structure if you take a look on the Web site—is painted bright orange, just in case anyone might have missed it.

Rule #3: *Promote Your Key Differentiators*

Picking up and delivering dry cleaning to homes and offices was Paul's best-known feature and a benefit that set him apart. It was, and remains, the foundation of his business. What will be your differentiator? As the years went by, Paul realized he had to plant other features in the public mind as other firms started copying his innovations. How could he get one step ahead of the market again? Answer: Emphasize another key innovation or activity. Paul was already specializing in shirts—an area with premium margins and a regular clientele in the business community—so he made shirt cleaning his number-one priority. He decided to offer not just final hand finishing, but other special touches, too. If customers had special requests, Prime Valet would oblige.

He also raised his prices, which nobody seemed to notice. Customer service standards also reached new heights. Paul says, "Even if one guy spent $10 a month, he still got good service—because you never know what his neighbor might be spending. He might well see a Prime Valet delivery truck stop next door."

Rule #4: *Launch Laser Beam Marketing Campaigns*

At some point a Bootstrapper must ask him- or herself: "Do I really need a marketing manager?" The answer is usually no, not during the early part of the business' life. For any start-up, those precious marketing dollars have got to go a very long way if they are to make any difference to the bottom line. Direct marketing can be very cheap and very cost effective. You need only create a decently designed leaflet on a PC, using a $69 version of Microsoft's Publisher. Pay for copying, and then spend some pleasant Sunday mornings walking around distributing them in local neighborhoods.

Even the smallest of start-ups, in even a mainstream yet highly competitive business such as dry cleaning, can make a real difference with clever marketing. Find a partner company or institution that puts you closely in touch with a large local market of people who are your ideal customer prospects. Take time choosing your partner in order to get it absolutely right.

Paul chose no less a partner than Delta Airlines, which had a large hub at Cincinnati Airport. In fact, some 65 percent of passengers passing through the airport flew with Delta. Paul set up a loyalty program with the airline based on frequent flier miles. He kept it simple: For every $1 customers spent with Prime Valet, they got one sky mile in return. Frequent fliers—middle managers, regional officers, and salespeople—wear lots of shirts and ties, so they were Paul's ideal targets. The scheme produced quick results. "Our typical frequent-flier customer spends 75 percent more than a conventional client," says Paul. So successful was the promotion, Delta decided to use Prime Valet as a case study example of how partnerships could work between large companies such as itself—and tiny firms like Paul's.

Rule #5: Reward Your Top 20 Percent

The benefits of the oft-mentioned rule of "80-20"—in which 80 percent of your business comes from 20 percent of your clients—should be maximized through marketing. Each year, Paul sends out gift certificates to his 100 best customers, offering $25 toward a meal at an upscale chain of Cincinnati restaurants. Prime Valet is charged only on redemption, which often comes in around $1,700, indicating that a high percentage (almost 70%) of customers take advantage of the offer and surely appreciate the gesture.

If 40 percent of your business comes from your top 5 to 20 percent of customers, giving those customers a token of your gratitude can lock in half of your annual business with them, suggests Paul. And while Paul spends only 2 percent of his revenues on marketing, it has been extraordinarily effective. Most dry-cleaning businesses spend around 7 percent.

Rule #6: Track Down Those "Nodal" Customers

What is a "node"? It's like an upturned umbrella that catches lots of raindrops and makes them flow naturally into a central point. A node for your company catches fresh orders and pours them into your business. Paul put a lot of effort into thinking about what organizations and institutions might be in a position to directly send him hundreds of new customers. He mulled over local universities and similar big institutions, the obvious candidates, but then came across "Best upon Request," a concierge services company that ran the concession for BankOne Towers, a massive apartment complex in Cincinnati with 1,600 tenants. The manager, David Lima, was impressed by Prime Valet's service and he opened the floodgates. Within a matter of weeks this one source of customers made up 10 percent of Paul's whole business. "For many businesses that's the difference between success and failure. It was so important in those early days," says Paul. Finding nodal customers is an exercise the Bootstrapper should also spend some time considering. As Paul so profitably proved, if you can come up with one or two organizations that can provide a channel of business, you'll do extremely well.

Rule #7: Don't Forget Social Network Marketing

Choosing just the right networks to tap into for your business promotion requires some forethought and diligent planning. You can waste evenings and weekends in the wrong circles. Some social networks will be useful, many not. Some focus on the golf club crowd, the local chamber of commerce groups, or just their own professional contacts. Going for new markets—the speciality of the Bootstrapper—almost always requires you to step outside your existing circles into new and strange social territories. So think about going where your competitors have never been, and would not think of going. This is what Paul Szydlowski did when he pushed Prime Valet into working closely with charities. For a fraction of the cost of conventional marketing, Paul got involved with as many charitable functions and fund-raisers as he could. Sports events (lots of cleaning there), black tie galas (yes, more cleaning here), church events (best outfits to be worn), festivals, and charity auctions were his targets. All agreed to put his leaflets into their guest take-away folders. The result: the biggest boost in Paul's business.

"No one was cynical about responding as they might have been with doorstep leafleting," he says. "They distributed many thousands of leaflets—straight into new customers' hands—through the gift packs and dinner table folders, all with lots of goodwill generated toward us as one of the sponsors."

No one likes to be cornered by an "entrepreneur on the make." "First build relationships, then revenues," advises Paul. Start with the biggest economic and social communities first. Local chambers of commerce have hundreds, often thousands of members. Let them know you exist. Use chamber of commerce notice boards, e-newsletters, and print journals to announce your arrival. Preferential treatment is often given out by chamber member companies to other member companies. In time, this semi-regular flow of sales can become your corporate bedrock. Second,

Paul quietly targeted local schools in his promotional work. Why? Because schools contain thousands of students whose parents are frequently involved in school activities at all levels. This meant that he was introduced to lots of parents who needed regular, high-quality cleaning services, and this relationship was achieved via a classic, soft-sell, noncorporate approach—via a friendly handshake at a school event.

Rule #8: Take Advantage of Day-to-Day Marketing

People like uniforms, even casual ones. They lend an air of authority and competence to the wearer. All of Prime Valet's staff wear either polo shirts or T-shirts or button-down shirts at work. Perhaps polo shirts are too common nowadays, and the astute Bootstrapper should think of something different. If your clientele is local, get your staff to put company bumper stickers on the back and both side windows of their vehicles. These can be very eye-catching. If you have a staff of twenty, for example, and half drive to work, your details will be seen by hundreds of commuters on a daily basis. More people remember a Web site address than they do a phone number, so find a catchy one. Also, if necessary, add a one-liner to the bumper stickers that explains what you do. This is all about visibility and clarity.

Rule #9: Get VIP Endorsements

Product endorsements from well-known people cut a great deal of ice with customers and reviewers. When Alasdair McLean-Foreman started HDO Sports, a Web site that provided a wide range of cool-looking sports equipment and accessories, his main market was middle-class male amateur runners. He launched a Web site with a hi-tech feel, and he later opened a sports shop in Boston. Slowly, he expanded his merchandise to include sunglasses, running shoes, and other items. Alasdair kept track of customers who bought running shoes so that he could e-mail them a personal reminder around four months later, when a serious runner would be in need of a new pair.

Searching for a marketing idea that couldn't be easily copied by competitors, Alasdair hit on the idea of sponsoring a group of elite Olympic athletes. Being an international athlete in the recent past, he had no difficulty finding suitable candidates. He then invited his customers to contact these athletes online—which they did by the hundreds. "The chance to engage in live online chat with a real athlete was compelling," says Alasdair. "They were thrilled, and it gave us lots of impact." The middle-class males loved to buy on the advice of star athletes, who also gave them free training advice at the same time. "We maximized our celebrity with fellow athletes," he said, "so we tried to give a level of service that Olympic athletes would expect."

Rule #10: Find Your Sector VIPs

Only a few people, often around a dozen, command influence over others in a particular market sector. These people are core opinion makers whom everyone else will listen to and respect. A very effective marketing move is to inform this handful of people that your company has just signed a major customer. It is probably unwise to contact these people too early in your start-up stage. Wait till you have a significant announcement to declare, or else they might think you're simply trying to "trampoline" off their reputation or worse, waste their time.

Rule #11: Stay Loyal to Your Earliest Customers

The customers who've been with you longest should be among your most valued customers. It's easy to forget them once your business is up and running, especially if they bought your product when it was a lot cheaper than it is today. But remember: You owe them. They bought your product when you most needed their business—and when you were at your most vulnerable.

They might have paid $1,000 instead of the $10,000 you're now getting from other companies, but they took a risk, perhaps a big risk in buying from you—so go that extra mile for them.

Rule #12: Stick with Your Strategy

Don't desert the marketplace where you have the most impact. Prime Valet has resolutely stuck with its niche business of cleaning shirts perfectly. And it has never strayed. Very often, companies spread themselves too thin and then fail. Mike Myer, RightNow's head of product development, says, "Some entrepreneurs try to be all things to all men. Instead, in a start-up, focus on the one area where your product is robust."

Rule #13: Put Your Best Foot Forward on the Web

In the modern world, your Web site could well be your primary calling card. Everyone uses sites to do some research on unknown newcomers such as yourself, long before you know they're tracking you or met them face-to-face. Your Web site, therefore, is crucial. It must contain relevant and timely information, and provide a complete introduction to your company. Ensure it's kept up to date—all the time.

Fancy designs are rarely worth the effort. Today, Web site excellence is all about content, not flashy graphics and music. The last two are infuriating to busy businesspeople. Keep your contact details on the front page on the top left or right, in significantly large type. Don't forget—up to a third of the people surfing the Web are simply looking for a contact phone number.

College students are forever on the lookout for small companies for whom they can produce very satisfactory Web sites for $200. Let them construct basic, eye-pleasing, well-structured pages that answer basic questions the general customer might have. Personalize it by putting your photo and those of your employees on the site. Give first-time callers the impression they are dealing with a professional, personable person—you. Lastly, take advantage of free listing and referral sites appropriate for your industry. The more Web sites that carry links to your site, the more traffic you will receive, and the more likely you are to appear high up in search engine listings.

Online Marketing

For Web-based companies, online marketing is a real opportunity if it is targeted in the right way to the right niche of prospects. Kim Scurry was the first marketing employee to be hired at RightNow Technologies, the twentieth employee up to then. Like many Internet-focused companies, RightNow began its marketing with conventional ideas. It placed an ad in *PC Week* magazine at a cost of $12,000. But one thing RightNow inaugurated was a system to track, even micromeasure, the effectiveness of every single marketing initiative. "We set up a Web site to monitor feedback from the *PCWeek* advert," said Kim, "but [the ad] didn't pay off."

Next, RightNow tried "fax blasts"—faxes sent off to several thousand recipients—and discovered the practice is illegal in several states. It also tried direct mail, banner ads on Web sites, and attending trade shows. Luckily, RightNow's tracking systems told it that direct mail, the Web ads, and trade shows were all ineffective or inefficient in producing leads given the costs involved. (As a side note to Bootstrappers: when involved in Web marketing, look out for the shoals of consultants and students who reply to your ads but are either eager to sell their own services or just want to engage in tire-kicking or other time-wasting activities.) In another move, RightNow tried a series of seminars, but found it difficult to get people to attend.

At every stage, RightNow established a specific Web site that monitored activity for every activity, so that it could judge how effective each one had been. If these leads later bought the product, no matter how much later, RightNow always knew its source. "Over the last three years we've tracked every lead from source to sale or to a dead end," says Kim. Her main advice to the Bootstrapper is: "Don't spend money on marketing activities that you can't measure, and secondly, try lots of different sorts of marketing—don't slavishly copy what your competitors are doing."

So what did work eventually?

1. RightNow started a series of Web casts, which were much less costly and involved less effort than a seminar series. To their joy, they found that these became popular.

2. RightNow gave away its software to popular Web sites on the understanding that RightNow would be allowed to name the sites as users in a press release, or that the sites would agree to receive not more than two calls per month from prospective RightNow customers looking for a reference. A "Powered by RightNow" Web link was also easily visible—and brought lots of leads.

3. Without any doubt, the key marketing technique that worked far better than any other was good customer references. The company invested in a core group of customers who were its best fans and allies. The group was named the "Inner Circle." "If a Bootstrapper can find a core of your 'product champions,' your earnest cheerleaders, that's a great start," says Kim Scurry. "They might tell a dozen other companies about how good you are."

4. Internet-based advertising can work brilliantly. Today around 70 percent of RightNow's marketing budget is spent on just two Web-based methods. "We're amazed our competitors haven't adopted them," says Kim. "The conversion-to-lead costs are very favorable."

On the first Web site, RightNow paid for an advertisement in certain e-newsletters that were well read. The ad was simplicity itself. It showed just five lines, and often didn't name RightNow at all. Instead, the text offered readers free access to a "white paper" on, for example, the "Top Ten Secrets of Customer Service." There was no sales pitch in the adverts. "We called back people who responded," says Kim, "sometimes even before they had left the site." Another method was to inform customers and prospects about Webinars, online sessions informing them about new technology.

The second Web-based method was "opt-in e-mail," where a company can buy or rent a list of names, and offer them access to one of the white papers. This soft-sell approach proved highly effective.

Shows and Exhibitions

Think carefully about what you want to achieve before spending money to exhibit at a trade show. Attending a show as an exhibitor is way beyond the budget of the average Bootstrapper, and it is time-consuming and usually ineffective in helping you meet the sort of quality contacts you need. Very often you'll find that many people at the show are casual visitors, students, and consultants who want to sell *you* something. Booth spaces can cost thousands of dollars, and people often feel pressure to pay for the same expensive 20 x 20 foot stand their competitors brought along. Granted, going to a trade show with a significantly smaller stand can damage your credibility, but on the other hand if you do pay for a booth, it means a large chunk of your workforce is out of the office for a week—and not selling.

A trade show can provide value for your money if it's the kind of show where all the exhibitors conduct business at the same-size "tabletop" booths. This feature puts everyone on an equal footing, and the cost to exhibit at such an event is typically under $300.

Another idea, if you're set on exhibiting at a trade show, is to ask a lead vendor to allow you to use some space in its booth. You might be one of several "junior" vendors, and it is likely that you might be asked to confine your sales to one market area, such as manufacturing. Given that your presence would require only one or two staff members, at modest cost, the results can sometimes be worth the time and money.

Making the Most of Trade Shows

For the Bootstrapper starting out, there might be a time when attending a key trade show could pay off. If you know that "Absolutely Everyone Who Matters" in your industry will be at a certain event, and you can't think of another way of making a quick entrance into your sector, then it might be worth the effort. Entry as a delegate isn't cheap. If you can afford a day rate fee—often the cheapest—it can set you back $300.

So how should you tackle it? First and foremost, you've got to make the very most of your day. Try to get the attendee list in advance. Pinpoint the most interesting people who might be future prospects. Your problem now is: How do I meet them all? The answer is to get up early, and get to the venue at least sixty minutes before it officially opens. Take up a position about 20 yards behind the attendee enrollment desk. As each attendee arrives, checks in, and walks past you, look at the name badge. Is this someone on your "hit list"? If so, grab him or her!

It is extremely useful to meet these senior executives and get a few moments of "face time" with them. If you're new and keen on making a mark on your sector, the executives will often be interested to hear what you have to say. Make your case quickly and concisely, exchange business cards, and ask if you might call him or her in a few days or the following week for a brief chat to take things further. When face-to-face, most human beings say "Yes."

Remember, you have a only few moments to impress. Make them count. Express yourself calmly, carefully, and informally but with purpose. Avoid excessive hand gestures, and avoid getting too close to people in your surge of enthusiasm.

Over the next hour or two, standing at your watch post, you'll get to meet more people and shake more hands than anyone except politicians and the U.S. president himself. By the end of it you should have pockets bulging with key contacts—all of whom have met you in person. Here's a tip: if you have time, try to note down on each card a few personal and business details that will help you remember the person you've met. Some will be positive, some not, but all must be detailed. These notes might be things like: "VIP: tall, distinguished, likes soccer—see again," or "First-rate prospect: call in two weeks." Sometimes it helps to note a person's physical details to aid memory.

When you call them back, these contacts are likely to remember you—or at least pretend they do. If the contacts had never met you, they would not in all probability take your call. This is why some trade shows can be of exceptional value for those Bootstrappers, especially raw beginners, whose business is very Spartan on prospects and requires a superconcentrated form of networking that might lead to an accelerated flow of contact "possibles." Of course, some won't subsequently take your call, but those who do will be strong candidates as customers.

Business Cards

Okay, you must take with you 200 or more business cards. Yes, really. Nothing looks more embarrassing and unprofessional than a businessperson who has forgotten or run out of cards. We all do it, but Bootstrappers can't afford to, certainly not during the early days. Your business card says an awful lot about you—good, bad, or indifferent.

The most common error made in business cards—and a potentially fatal mistake for the Bootstrapper—is that around

50 percent fail to tell the reader what service is being offered. It might sound hard to believe, but it's true. Look through your business cards and see how many have a short description about a professional activity. If you work for GE, Rolls-Royce, or Boeing, this matters less. But for the Bootstrapper it's crucial.

Put "Cleaning Services for Every Sector," or "Home Meals for the Healthcare Industry" on yours. Once you get going, you can even consider adding the names of key customers—with their permission, of course. If you're a supplier to Siemens, even to a subsidiary part of Siemens, or to your local memorial hospital, or to any other institution of note, consider adding it near the bottom of your card. It looks impressive.

A second giveaway is the quality of the paper. Today, with modern printing facilities at rock-bottom prices, there is no excuse for printing business cards on cheap, bendy paper. Such cards look cheap and nasty because they *are* cheap and nasty. Card means card. Specify that you want a stiff card, and if you can afford raised type, specify that, too. Your business card should do everything to convince your contacts that you are anything but an amateur.

Avoid shiny cards, if only because it prevents people from writing notes about you on them. Large, nonstandard, or folding cards just seem egotistic, and because they won't fit easily with standard cards, they are more liable to be thrown away than kept. Avoid plastic cards—the corners and edges cut like razorblades.

Lastly, type size. Many business cards use tiny type. That's ridiculous. With our steadily aging population, the last thing you want to do is to tax the eyesight of your clientele. Keep key details such as your name and phone number in large, emboldened type.

In some countries, such as Germany, business cards often include a photo, which aids identification. In the United States, photo cards are more common in the creative industries than in more mainstream businesses.

A Clear Strategy

The bottom line for marketing is to be clear about your strategy. Far too many small companies are blown in all directions by market forces. But proficient marketing will prevent a small firm from becoming isolated and getting all of its answers internally. Even though you will be drawn here and there, keep to your marketing plan. Inevitably, the proportion of your marketing that is conducted via leaflets and in person will vary depending on the results of your Web-based marketing activities. Above all, try to reach as big a market as early on as you can.

a bootstrapping exercise

Ask yourself the following questions about your business:

- What market should we target with our new products?
- Whom should I form alliances and partnerships with?
- Where is the market moving to next?

CHAPTER 10

MAKING THE PRESS
WORK FOR YOU

"Get your facts first, and then you can
dust them off as much as you please."

—*Mark Twain*

Increasingly, getting noticed by the press is the single most
important marketing boost for small companies. The problem
of "being unknown" is one of the biggest business headaches
for a large number of Bootstrapped firms with products that are
ready to go. Markets don't know you exist; customers have never
heard of you. Public relations agencies are too far expensive, and
mainstream advertising is ineffective.

However, just one appearance in the press can dramatically
change your fortunes, and in the long term it can result in a big
improvement to your bottom line. In fact, a significant number
of media-savvy small companies have built their futures on the
foundation of comprehensive media coverage. A few well-placed
profiles in the media can do more for your business than a thousand recommendations. Many leading businesspeople look upon

their relationship with the press as an integral part of their business careers. And so must you. In truth, business journalists have an endless lust for "success stories," so however minor your success might seem, know that it has real publicity value. Best of all, a single article is frequently picked up by dozens of other media organizations that run it with little amendment. One story in the newspaper has the potential to spread like wildfire into other newspapers, magazines and newsletters, and across Web sites, radio, and TV.

Certain publications are much more important than others, and you have to identify which publications are the most widely read by your potential customers and have the biggest influence over them. In each sector, the opinions of a handful of journalists have greater significance than the opinions of the rest of their colleagues. Track down this set of journalists and let them know you've got something to say. Once you've developed a relationship with each of these key journalists, they will look to you for news, features, quotes, and statements in the future.

Getting Journalists to Pay Attention

Fundamentally, a Bootstrapper should first understand what drives most journalists: the need to fill column inches. The shortage of high-quality stories is an endless worry. Some reporters lie awake at night wondering how they are going to fill tomorrow's broadcast or the next edition of the publication. The majority of journalists are overworked and underpaid, so make life easy for them, and you'll reap the benefits. This is your opportunity but good timing is key. Why? Often journalists get up early, are out all day interviewing and researching, and arrive back at the office at 4 P.M. Only then do they sit down to start writing. They often don't get home till after 9 P.M.

The worst thing you can do is to cold-call when deadlines

loom. In the late afternoon, journalists are busy writing and editing the day's set of pages. Feature writers are often asked to write 1,500 words on an emerging news story in under two hours; radio journalists often have minutes in which to write a script before a broadcast. Mornings are usually best, though many journalists have a daily content conference, often at 11 A.M.

Before you contact the press, think very carefully about what might make a good story. Few Bootstrappers have asked themselves this question, but this is the number-one starting point of your media "career." Analyze carefully the most interesting and arresting aspects of your business, and decide what it is about *your* business that would make an interesting story. The fact that you've started a new business is not a good enough news story, because dozens of people do this every day. But if your business produced a groundbreaking product or process—that's news. Is it unique? What are the likely benefits? Ask yourself: What are we doing that is faster, neater, cleaner, sweeter, and meaner than anyone else? Is it an example of a growing trend? All Bootstrappers live a rollercoaster of highs and lows, of small victories and disappointments. Remember these incidents, and include them as humorous or serious anecdotes to add essential color to future stories. A golden rule is that you should contact a journalist only when you have a story that you are sure *the journalist*—not you— will think is interesting. Imagine your story in the publication you are calling—Would an average reader want to read it? That is how you know if you have something truly newsworthy.

Learning about the Media

You might not know any journalists just yet. Libraries and online directories provide exhaustive lists of print and other media outlets of all kinds. Read those papers and magazines and watch the key Web sites that your target market reads most.

a bootstrapper's tale:

Getting the Word Out

One of the most remarkable and unlikely business stories of the past ten years has been the extraordinary rise of PrintingForLess.com, the online print-ordering service started by Andrew Field, a Bootstrapper in Livingston, Montana. He more than anyone knows how important media coverage has been in giving his business a worldwide reputation. But Andrew never used a public relations firm. Instead he approached the media at every opportunity and gave them a fact-filled summary of the burgeoning progress of his business. It worked.

Journalists at the *Billings Gazette* and the *Denver Post* soon became aware that they had a world leader on their doorstep. Articles in leading business and innovation magazines such as *Forbes* and *Inc.* followed quickly. This media coverage gave the tiny company massive nationwide coverage. Tens of thousands of small companies that couldn't afford professional designers heard about Andrew's company for the first time, and jammed his site with orders.

A second flood of interest erupted when an article appeared in Microsoft's *Business Advantage* magazine. PrintingForLess had successfully written software that enabled computer files, written in Microsoft's Publisher program, to be linked with printers via the PrintingForLess Web site. International press coverage followed, and now the company is receiving orders from many parts of the world.

For Andrew, the press played a major role in turning a small print business based in Montana into a world-recognized brand.

Note the names of individual journalists. Many now put their e-mail addresses at the end of articles and on free e-mail newsletters produced by magazines and Web sites focusing on your chosen business sector.

Note the subjects the journalists cover, especially if they seem to like stories about innovation and enterprise, because this is your niche. If entrepreneurship is not well covered, look for journalists who concentrate on technology innovation, small business, or new start-ups. Figure out whether your story might make a good business news story, a features section story, or a story for more specialized areas such as finance, manufacturing, the Internet, franchising, or new products and services.

Being a bare-knuckle Bootstrapper who's created a thriving business with little capital is not necessarily interesting in itself. But you can make it sound much more interesting by the way you describe it. Presentation is everything. Make it sound like an adventure, a "high-risk, all-or-nothing" story, without straying from the truth. A slice of drama goes a long way.

Talking to the Trade Press

Perhaps the quickest way of creating a relationship with journalists, especially those working on trade publications, is to send them an e-mail. If you've read an article that impressed you in some way, dispatch an e-mail giving the journalist your comments. E-mail is probably the world's most common method of opening contact with a complete stranger.

If your comments are based on your hard-won business experience, you'll almost certainly get a reply. Your experience might well strike a chord with the journalist, especially if your comments are short and sharp, and contain one or two relevant facts. At this point your dialogue is unfolding.

In your second e-mail, suggest that you and the journalist have a talk on the phone. When that phone call takes place the journalist will know in advance that you won't be wasting his or her time. The journalist might well find your views both original and realistic. Give him or her a quick profile of your company—just the headline facts and never a torrent of detail. Then it is very likely that the journalist will put you on a "hit list" of companies to write about in the future.

On and Off the Record

In the past, journalists made firm distinctions between facts, opinions, and comments that could be published and those that could not—those conversations were deemed "off the record." Today, it's best to assume that there is no such thing as off the record. Be aware that anything you say to a journalist might well end up in the press, with your name next to it. For that reason you must maintain a degree of discretion about confidential matters concerning your business—which you should do in any case. No matter how friendly and personable your relationships with journalists become, be sure to maintain discretion and caution with your comments.

Calling the Newspaper

If you prefer a direct approach, you can phone the business desk of the particular publication and ask to speak to the journalist who broadly covers your business sector. Usually the phone is answered by the junior editorial assistant or the desk secretary. Getting through to the business editor is often difficult unless he or she already knows you.

You might have news of a major new contract or a significant investment from a business angel. Always add a relevant fact—"factoid," as journalists call it. Sound authoritative. Then when you get a journalist on the phone, you literally have three or four sentences—max—to impress the journalist that your story is of interest to the public and to the journalist. Choose your opening sentences with care. Write them out beforehand and repeat them to yourself once or twice. If you read the first two or three sentences of news stories in a paper, you'll soon get a grip on how to present your story quickly and fluently. It doesn't hurt to start the conversation with a little flattery. "I've been reading stories with your byline for some weeks, and I enjoyed your coverage of that new product [whatever it was] last month." Then start your spiel.

Almost any story can be told from a variety of different "angles." You can lead with a mention of a new contract or a statement about the main benefits of your product or service. If your business is doing something surprising and novel, state what it is clearly and succinctly. If yours is a news story, offer the journalist several important news aspects—for example, what's novel about your business, what are you offering that's against the trend. Offer a quick anecdote from your business experience if it backs up your story.

Is your story linked to an event happening that day, tomorrow, or on the weekend? Use superlatives where possible, and where justified. Tell the journalist: "We're the fastest-growing business in our sector" or "Our product is faster, more effective, and offers significant advantages over our big-name competitor." You can also offer your story as an exclusive to a particular journalist.

Do everything you can do to make your story accurate. We can't emphasize the importance of accuracy too strongly. Newspapers are littered with minor but annoying errors—usually due to miscommunication. It would be a disaster if your name and your company's were misspelled in your first article. It often happens. To avoid this, spell out your name in full, and that of your company—don't expect the journalist to do it correctly—especially if your name is unusual or open to error. Are you a Mr. Howarth, or Haworth? Are you a Ms. Johnson, Johnston, or Johnstone? Over the phone these names sound similar. Names beginning with Bs and Ps can sound identical, too. Fs are often heard as Ss. Another tip: If you name a staff member in a press release who is called Alex, Sam, or Chris—names commonly used by both sexes—make clear early on whether he or she actually is a she or a he.

State your job title, but keep titles brief. Journalists are never too keen on long titles because they take up too much space. For Bootstrappers, "founder and CEO" is sufficient, but even as your business grows you shouldn't allow your managers to give out titles such as "Vice President, Corporate Marketing, Photocopier Sales and Service, Western States Region." Shorten any such titles for the journalist. In print these long titles can look self-important—something you want to avoid. Journalists often want to print your age. Don't take offense: It's vital for the reader to know how old you are. State your age openly, and your peer group will warm to you.

After your conversation, send an e-mail (prepare one in advance so you can respond quickly) that briefly summarizes your story's main aspects in bullet point form. Make your summary easy to understand, and explain any little-known technical words where necessary. You should send this e-mail to keep your name in front of the journalist and to provide a brief reminder of the message you want to get out. But wait—don't disappear after the interview, because it's not over yet! The journalist might need to phone you again to ask a last-minute question before your article goes to print. Often, a vital fact has been left out.

Caution: Never ask, let alone insist, that the journalist submit an article to you for approval before it is printed. For a journalist to do would get him or her fired in most news organizations. However, where there is controversy involved, you can ask—as a condition of providing the interview—that all of your quotes in the piece will be read to you over the phone prior to publication. Tell the journalist that you don't want to alter the article's editorial content, but want to identify your own verbal errors, and highlight any opportunities for clarification. We frequently speak in rather loose phrases that do not express what we truly want to say. The real thought might have been in our head at the time but we failed to express it properly. We all do this.

If you don't get the chance to give an interview, you can send a fully detailed press release, again via e-mail. One tip: Send it as plain text in the body of the e-mail. Avoid attachments, particularly PDFs, because life is too short to wait for the PDF file to open. Put your name, e-mail address, and phone number at the top of the text. Most press releases include a quote, so if you include one, keep it to only one quote from one person. Some releases contain quotes from three or four company staff—the CTO, the COO, the founder, and the marketing director—which becomes totally confusing. Stick to one individual (yourself best of all) and don't dilute your message.

Have Photos Ready

Having your own set of photos is vital. Newspapers and magazines are unlikely to send out a photographer across the city just to take pictures of a minor story on your company. But if you have those photos ready you've got a much greater chance of getting your story in the paper.

At the end of every phone interview with a journalist, never fail to ask if he or she wants photos or some form of artwork from you. Don't expect the journalist to ask you—journalists often forget or leave it to the picture desk to contact you later. Ask for the name and e-mail address of the picture editor or the picture desk staff member who deals with your journalist's section of the paper, and send the photos directly to that person.

Some photo editors favor a certain format, often a wide-angle shot showing some of your company's staff holding your products close to the camera. Where possible, be clever about it. Try to get your company's Web site address in the photo because, unfortunately, not all media like to print or broadcast this key detail. For example, get your staff to wear T-shirts with the URL clearly visible. Also, try to have available one high-quality, high-resolution digital color photo each of yourself, your colleagues, your product, and whatever else might be eye-catching about your business.

Don't forget to write a caption for all your photos, especially where they show a group of people who need to be identified by name and job title. For example, this might read: "John Smith (far left), CEO, is holding our compact new product while Jim Jones, marketing manager (second right), holds the much larger, older product we first launched back in 2003."

Moving from News to Features and Beyond

In spite of all your efforts, your story might not appeal to a particular journalist. So always, always ask the journalist to recommend the name of another journalist on the paper, or even a different paper, who might be more excited about it.

A news journalist might recommend contacting the features desk at the same paper, because your story might be more interesting as an in-depth item, rather than a piece of straight news. Again, tell the features journalist why your story is revealing and relevant. Suggest fundamental themes. Offer at least one hard, interesting fact about your business, and explain why this is significant. Have you remembered to add that pithy, humorous anecdote? Could your story make an interesting corporate profile or a personality piece? Does the journalist have a series of articles coming up—on new business innovation, new business processes, or new emerging faces in business—where your story might be of interest?

Most Bootstrappers are unlikely to be making a product or process that will make it into the front few news pages. But there are important exceptions. If your product or service has a direct link to a major news story, call the news desk directly. For example, in Europe more than 200 passengers suffocated in a tragic fire onboard a ferry. Most were found within 20 feet of an exit because they just couldn't see their way out. A small company that produces special acoustic alarms that guide people to an exit in darkness or smoke-filled conditions contacted the press. "If this type of sound alarm had been fitted, there would be little doubt that many of those who perished would have survived," they explained. In subsequent days the product received global coverage.

The Right Timing

Occasionally, it's best to bide your time with the press. A Bootstrapper's story might get only a few lines in the business pages of a newspaper, but it could receive much more space in the regular business supplements that papers and magazines produce. These supplements can be sector specific (IT/software, business services, or raising capital) and appear irregularly, or more general and appear weekly, monthly, or quarterly. Make a note of when these and other types of supplements appear. In addition to business magazines, special editions for the holidays and Christmas are often printed and might cover, for example, consumer goods that you as the Bootstrapper might be producing. Regular supplements could include sections devoted to the needs of older people (opticians, medical devices, and homecare needs) or to the needs of children (child care, schooling, and healthcare).

Provide Additional Contacts

If you can cut the time it takes for a journalist to write your piece—do it—because he or she will appreciate your efforts. A journalist must consult a variety of sources to provide a "balanced and informed" view of your product and company, so having additional contacts is always very useful. If a journalist can find all in one place all the opinions needed for an article, that's a very economic use of his or her time.

Here's your chance to provide the journalist with those contacts—in this case, a shortlist of your most valued customers. Have those customers ready and waiting by telling them well in advance that a journalist might be calling them. Comments from your contented customers makes your company credible to readers. If your product offers a technical or scientific advantage, find an industry analyst or other respected third party who will give your product what is known as "independent verification." Remember: The journalist has no idea whether your product is the best or worst, but he or she can arrive at a view by speaking to experts whose names you've conveniently provided.

Staging Stunts

Many small businesses try to arrange amusing events and offers that will attract local press interest. Bootstrappers enjoy harmless stunts, and so do the media. If you're a caterer, for example, ask the local university if you can teach a group of freshmen how to cook. This will give you the opportunity to sell to the university later, or provide it with a regular supply of precooked food, or cater for large student parties in the future. When you fix the date for your stunt, invite the press along.

If you're a cleaning company, you can offer to clean up the "messiest student room on campus," and have a press photographer take photos of the before and after. Universities usually employ a photographer, so you can usually obtain some free photos from him or her later.

Become an Expert Speaker

Many organizations are on the lookout for new and interesting speakers. At every opportunity, volunteer to give a speech.

The subject doesn't have to be about your business, not at first anyway. It might be about your market sector's general prospects, innovations, successes, market trends, and other related topics. Impress the audience, and leave them with the impression that you are thoughtful, insightful, and charismatic.

The main aim is to make people like you. At every event at which you speak, get hold of the attendee list for your future marketing purposes. If you were well received by the audience, the people who hear you speak will be much more likely to welcome a sales call from you in the future. Soon you will be seen as a business "personality" and a business leader by your local media and business community.

You'll be nervous at first, but after speech number three or four, the nerves die away. When you first start out on the speaking circuit, rehearse your speeches in front of a group of friends, family, or colleagues. This practice will greatly sharpen your speaking skills. Make your speech lively. Start and end with a joke (preferably about yourself), and leave them laughing. Listen to great speakers such as Winston Churchill who made it seem easy. Churchill wrote his lines on cards in three-line sequences, and rehearsed his speeches over and over again. Copy his method, if it works for you.

Entrepreneurs who make themselves available, who smile a lot and have a supply of anecdotes and witticisms, are the darlings of the modern business media. The combination of personal flair, fluent speaking, attractive appearance, and business success remains a huge draw for the press. Entrepreneurs such as Michael Dell of Dell Computers and many others like him have gained tremendous business advantage from their media presence. Watch them on TV, and see how they do it. Observe how they handle difficult questions. It is their example you'll need to follow.

a bootstrapper's tale:

For the Love of Pizza and Beer

ometimes a really clever stunt can work magnificently. Bootstrapper Lon McGowan's iClick digital camera business in Seattle had been in business only three weeks. A mass of e-mails had gone out, yet the phone was silent. Nobody seemed to have noticed his venture; no one in the media was interested. "Come back to us when you're a success," they said. Burdened with credit card debts of $25,000 and rising, Bootstrapper Lon was desperate to get some coverage to kick-start sales.

Scanning the front page of a newspaper one morning, Lon read about Geoff Tweeton and a friend who planned to stand outside a movie theater in Seattle for a full five months. They were determined to be first in the line to see the next *Star Wars* movie. Lon could already imagine other news reporters and photographers gathering at the scene after they read the story. At that moment, an idea hatched inside Lon's head.

Lon rushed down to the site and introduced himself. "I want to sponsor you," he said breathlessly, "but I've got no money." He promised the pair unlimited free pizzas and beer for a few weeks if they would wear iClick T-shirts, take pictures of passersby with iClick cameras, and have their own photos taken in front of iClick banners. Geoff and his friend agreed.

One by one the world's media organizations began covering Geoff's obsessive gesture. When a nationwide morning TV crew arrived, Geoff knew the time had arrived. The cameraman tried to move away from the banner bearing the iClick name in large letters, but Geoff pulled him back. "Listen everyone," he said, "just go take a look at this site." The cameraman moved away quickly, but within minutes, the iClick server was receiving thousands of hits from across America. That short exposure provided Lon McGowan with a flood of brand recognition. And the cost? Just $130 in pizzas, beer, and T-shirts.

From "Talking Head"
to Business Figurehead

If you know journalists are in the audience when you're making a speech, be sure you introduce yourself to them afterward. Meanwhile, during your speech, show yourself off as someone who has an opinion and is not afraid to express it. That's the kind of personality you are, and the kind journalists like to talk to. Now use this to your business advantage.

Once you meet the journalists, let them know that you are ready to provide quick and pertinent comments on a whole range of subjects. Again, these are not just business subjects but run the gamut of human activity—stories that cut across education, infrastructure, housing prices, lifestyle, travel, and sport. You name it: your choice of car, preferred ski resort, your source of business advice. Everyone likes to learn from the experiences and wisdom of seasoned, successful individuals—such as you.

If, for example, you've started a flourishing restaurant business, the newspaper's food writer or lifestyle editor might call you to ask about your customers' changing tastes this season. "What are they ordering?" you'll be asked. You're in the prime position to know—and to comment. And this is just the start. A journalist on the business desk might phone you if he's writing a "state of the nation" article, seeking to find out how well or badly the local or city economy is doing. Expenditure in restaurants is a good indicator of people's spending power and level of confidence. A journalist on the news desk might call after a food poisoning incident to ask you how a professional caterer deals with this issue, and other matters of best practice.

Don't forget, local city newspapers in the United States still have sizable readerships, often in the hundreds of thousands, and are well-respected by the reading public. Become a mouthpiece of informed opinion and always be honest. Don't exaggerate how well business is doing. If sales are down, say so. Don't be seen as a promoter of "good news" all the time. Leave that to some of the Wall Street analysts who forecast sunshine every day of the year. Be realistic, or in the end no one will believe you. In the long term, if your views turn out to be accurate, journalists will return time and again.

Enter Business Awards Programs

Each year hundreds of U.S. cities and dozens of states organize business and enterprise competitions, and so do national innovation magazines such as *Inc.* Many contests often have a "Best Newcomer" category—which is ideal for the budding Bootstrapper.

Awards categories include those events for best product innovation, best new enterprise, and companies with the highest growth rates. These are very media-friendly events. If you win an award, you also get free publicity. Journalists love awards events such as these because all the research work is usually done for them by the award sponsor, often including a table of companies showing their growth figures, along with stories and photos of the beaming winners. Even if you're short-listed and don't win, attend the awards event anyway and take a copy of the attendee list. It's more meat for your marketing efforts.

When your company is larger, you'll be ready to enter the regional and national Deloitte & Touche Fast 50 competitions, or the Ernst & Young Entrepreneur of the Year event. Some programs demand three years of results before your company can enter.

Putting Press Coverage to Good Use

Gaining good press coverage is just the start. Now put your efforts to good business use. First, log all of your significant press coverage and immediately add it to your Web site. Put any glowing praise or quotes into any leaflets or handouts you might be producing. Showcasing your press coverage not only reinforces your credibility among customers, it also reinforces your status among journalists who have not yet written about you. If one magazine or paper has covered you, don't be shy about contacting their media rivals.

Here are two final thoughts on getting the most out of press coverage. First, if you have any well-known clients—politicians, VIPs, sports stars, or well-liked (preferably noncontroversial) celebrities—ask their permission to mention their names in media interviews. In return, promise not to disclose any private personal or financial details at any point. Second, if any of your press coverage is particularly impressive, blow up the image size of the article (at Kinko's or any other copy center), mount it on card backing, and hang it on your office reception wall so every visitor gets to see it. It all adds to your corporate strength and reputation.

Indirect Opportunities for Media Exposure

Finally, often your best opportunity of getting your company into the press is when someone associated with your company is the prime focus of interest in an article. For example, your employees probably have a variety of interests and passions outside the office, ranging anywhere from sports to music to dance to chess to fund-raising to being an expert on a particular subject. One of them could capture the interest of the local press. And if he or she is photogenic, so much the better. If appropriate, get the employee to say he or she works for your company, to name it and add a brief superlative or explanatory factoid, and to state the URL. These tidbits frequently get published. For example, the article might say your employee works for "Good Food Inc, the city's newest home meal chain," or "currently the fastest-growing home meal service in the city." These are key statements readers remember.

UPS found a great way to get indirect press coverage by allowing its employees to take a lengthy time off to train for competition at the Olympic Games. In so doing, UPS secured many column inches of positive press that would otherwise have cost millions of dollars in advertising. A principal outlet for such stories is the oft-forgotten "human interest media"—those magazines that cover popular activities such as gardening, women's issues, fashion, photography, personal computing, digital cameras, and even entertainment, and which have giant readerships running into the hundreds of thousands.

Many of these human interest magazines hang around in doctors' and dentists' waiting rooms and the reception areas of hundreds of other businesses for months and years, far longer than newspapers, which gives longevity to any story written about your business or someone who works for you. If one of your staff is having an unusual wedding or is successful in a sport, for example, offer the story to one of these magazines. Magazines are keenly interested in individual success stories involving females, youthful executives, ethnic minorities, or new migrants to the United States.

a bootstrapping exercise

Make the following lists, and use them in your campaign for media attention:

- The ten most important publications read by your target customers
- The key journalists who most cover your particular sector in those publications
- The five most newsworthy aspects of your business
- The five elements of your business that would make a good photo

CHAPTER 11

STRESS-BUSTING STRATEGIES

"If you're going through hell, keep going."

—*Winston Churchill*

The effort required to build a business can be enormous, and you'll experience stressful moments when your patience and endurance are tested to the limit. The Bootstrapper can adopt a series of techniques to offset that pressure, so that eventually, you'll be able to handle anything.

Very often, the "disasters" that hit you yield extraordinary benefits that were totally invisible at the time. For example, let's say you just submitted your first significant contract, and it took you an entire day to prepare the 120-page bid document that included all those photocopies of insurance, legal, and business documents. Then it gets rejected out of hand in a two-line e-mail. And you feel crushed.

Later, you start to see the benefits of your misfortune. First, you learned the critical, core lesson of how to put together a comprehensive bid. This will be invaluable in the future. The next one should take much less time, perhaps only a few hours, to compile. Second, if you were bidding against near impossible opposition, your bid might have been weak, so perhaps you should not have been bidding at all. Third, you might have made a mistake, so check your offering against the company that won. Lastly, your rejection might lead you to rethink your strategy. Perhaps it's time to find a more realistic opportunity, a fresher market niche where your talents and your product offering can make much more of a difference.

The hard truth about business, and of course life in general, is that we truly learn only from the "shocks" in life. We're apt to learn little in the good times. Success merely reaffirms your belief in your strategy and your faith in the product, yet teaches you nothing. Tough times can teach all manner of useful lessons, and will make you into a much more battleworthy business player than you were before. Becoming battleworthy is the key to being a successful Bootstrapper.

Minimizing the Stress

Bootstrapping a business is undoubtedly stressful. But there are many ways to minimize the impact of stress and blunt the pressure that falls on you each day. Often you have to change your attitudes about work, but there's nothing wrong in that. Bootstrapping is a learning experience.

After three years of building his management consultancy, Tim Jenkins, the cofounder of Point B Solutions, thinks he has formulated an unbeatable set of stress-busting techniques. Some are purely practical. Others invite you to get your mental attitudes and disciplines in a straight line. All together Tim's advice can help you to always to be the victor rather the victim of stress.

Stress Buster #1: Make an Appointment with Exercise

"A Bootstrapper is like a farmer: Your work never ends," says Tim. "You could work eighteen hours a day, seven days a week, and you still won't feel like you've done enough." There is always something pressing that could provide an excuse not to exercise. Yet, exercise is a vital part of long-term success. "Your mind is much sharper when your body is tuned up," he remarked. "At the same time, exercise has proven biochemical, stress-relieving effects."

In the early days of Point B, Tim struggled with getting enough exercise. Every time he went to the gym, even on weekends, he found himself feeling guilty that he wasn't at his desk instead. But Tim persevered and found a pickup basketball game at his gym that took place three days a week at lunchtime. He started to schedule "basketball meetings" with friends at the gym. "And when I say schedule, I mean it," he said. "The appointments were right there in my Outlook Calendar."

Again, he felt guilty, so he kept his cell phone and pager at courtside. But over time, he realized nothing was going to happen between noon and 2 P.M. that he couldn't solve at 2:30.

Eventually, he set himself a work schedule, which he adhered to like clockwork, with a morning shift from 7 A.M. to noon, and an afternoon shift from 2 to 6 P.M. each day. These two shifts sandwiched his exercise time. Within days, he could feel a big difference in his performance and stress levels, between the days he exercised and the days he didn't.

Feeling guilty about taking time to exercise can be the razor's edge of stress. Remember: You're making yourself feel guilty. You are doing to yourself. So banish the guilt. The lesson is to build a schedule of exercise into your work pattern, and make it as regular a pattern of exercise as possible.

Stress Buster #2: Learn to Think Through Your Problems

Some of the most stressful moments in business happen when you can't find a solution to a problem that's bothering you. It is easy to worry about it, and difficult to stop worrying. But if you take firm steps to think through (rather than *worry* through) a problem, you'll find that elusive solution is much easier to see. Every problem has a solution. You just haven't thought hard enough about it—or you haven't spoken to the right people about it—yet. One successful executive says: "When I'm really stuck, I put my head in my hands for just five minutes, and eventually the solution comes to me."

If none of your employees has an answer, call a mentor or a trusted confidante. If that person can't help, widen your scope again. Send out an e-mail describing the problem in brief to a group of your closest contacts, asking them for imaginative advice. There is wisdom in having many advisers.

Stress Buster #3: Remember Why You're Doing This

You started your business in order to have a better life or a higher standard of living, to see the dream of your product on the market fulfilled, or to escape the corporate rat race and spend more time with your family. Keeping in mind your true motivation for starting your business will often help you to deal with the inevitable stress. You'll be much better able to deal with start-up stress because you'll see it as being a necessary part of achieving a very desirable end.

Stress Buster #4: Don't Let Big Issues Linger

Confront "the elephant in the room." It's human nature to want to avoid ugly tasks or issues, but they can drain your energy in both the short and long term if they are not addressed. If you have a problem employee or customer or a sticky business issue, don't let it fester. Face the problem early on and be prepared to take an initial hit in order to pave the way for longer-term productivity and peace of mind. You might experience the same feeling about a business problem as you did when you were back in college worrying about a term paper that was due in a few days. "Tackle it and get it done, and then enjoy yourself all the way up to the deadline," said Tim Jenkins.

Stress Buster #5: Take the Longer View

Don't get downcast by the disorganized nature of change. As a Bootstrapper you are striving to create something new every day. Change, innovation, and improvement always take time—often far more time than you predicted.

Just remember that the great majority of new, innovative, and highly successful projects in the world often appeared to be complete disasters halfway through the project. Think of the chaos, dirt, and confusion of a building site, and compare that with the perfection of a clean complete structure. In a Bootstrapped business, your life might seem as if you are living in a psychological building site. Try to accept this as normal.

Your customers won't see, and probably won't care about, the pain and trauma that went into the design of your product, but they will delight in its finished perfection and functionality. That's when you'll feel it was all worthwhile.

Stress Buster #6: Keep Your Focus

Too many budding entrepreneurs allow themselves to get sidetracked by the minutiae associated with running a growing business. There's a certain appeal to dealing with novel operational issues that you never had in your previous jobs. Setting up a local area network or buying office furniture can actually be an interesting distraction if you've never done it before.

Tim was rudely awakened to this fact by one of his partners one day early in Point B's existence. Tim had spent several hours the previous day comparing cell-phone plans, and proudly presented the findings to his two partners. "I had figured out a way to save a couple of thousand dollars a year on our bills," he recalls. After he had finished, his partner replied, "You know what? I think you need to get out and sell some more work." Tim was downhearted, but his partner was right. "We needed top-line growth," says Tim, "not cost reduction. The fact that we were overspending on cell phones was immaterial to our business success. We could deal with that issue later—once we had put some money in the bank!"

Stress Buster #7: Share the Workload

When you're under a heavy workload and tight deadlines, sometimes the hardest thing to do is hand over tasks to someone else with less experience. This requires more work initially, and your natural tendency is to spend an hour doing the work rather than fifty minutes teaching the person to do the task.

"Try to resist the temptation to do everything yourself and focus on the long term benefits of growing others around you," says Tim, "distributing a sense of ownership and accountability, and removing yourself from the center of all workflow in the organization." Let go of some of your most favored or sacred tasks. Train your staff until you can let them stand on their own. When you hire great people, sharing the workload is a lot easier.

Stress Buster #8: Make Sure Your Expectations Don't Exceed Your Requirements

When you start out as a Bootstrapper, every day you will feel as though you must pull out all the stops to get a job done. But, in reality, it's not the end of the world if you *don't* get it to the client by Friday.

It can be highly stressful when you just can't meet a deadline. In its early days, Point B often had so many projects at one time that everyone felt like plate spinners—they'd have to keep running from one project to another just to keep the whole show going. The way to ease that kind of stress is to always ask your client if a deadline is an absolute must or, as is much more common, just desirable. Tim says: "I would often ask a client: 'I know I can get this done by Friday, but would next week be possible?' Ninety-five percent of the time clients would say, 'Oh yes, no problem.'"

When you're having trouble making a deadline, don't always assume you need to do an all-nighter to satisfy the customer. You could give the customer a call and say, "I know you need 1,000 units on Friday. I can run around the clock to get them to you if you need them, but I could also deliver 500 on Friday and 500 more on Tuesday." This kind of conversation can also strengthen your relationship, changing it from merely a vendor-supplier link to a more personal tie.

If your customer holds you to the deadline the customer will usually appreciate the effort you make to satisfy your commitment. If your customer is flexible then you've found a way to relieve a stress point.

Stress Buster #9: Focus on Satisfying Your Customers

The first goal of a start-up is to create satisfied customers who are willing to pay you an acceptable price for your product or service. Tim agrees. "It is easy to set yourself lofty and misguided goals and then become absolute slaves to them," he says. Targets of "growing 30 percent this year," or to become "bigger than our chief competitor in two years," are all commendable, but far too many Bootstrappers feel they've failed and become depressed if they don't meet those goals.

If your goal was to grow 30 percent this year and it turns out to be only 25 percent, is that failure? It isn't if you never set a 30 percent goal in the first place. "Now I'm not saying that goals and targets don't have a role in growing a business," says Tim. "However, you must be careful not to set high expectations when you don't need to." Instead, you should have high expectations around cultivating and serving your customers. "If you set lofty goals here, the other numbers will often follow," Tim says. "At Point B we never had a business plan and we have never set any numeric goals. Nonetheless, we've enjoyed impressive success as we approach ten years in business. We did it by keeping our focus on our clients, and our own people as well."

Stress Buster #10: Keep Things in Perspective

No matter how bad things get or seem to get, you still have a life outside your work. "You have family and friends that care about you no matter how well or badly your business does," Tim argues. "You also have hobbies and interests that will not go away even if your business does." Make a point to spend time away from work focusing on the other important people and things in your life. "It's much less difficult keeping things in perspective when you do this," he points out.

Tim's son was born four days before Point B was formed. Tim's mother promptly removed him from being the executor of her will—shocked as she was by his "irresponsible" behavior in leaving a steady job to start a new business. But coming home every day and playing with his son, and later his daughter, helped Tim keep the events at his new business in perspective. "How bad can things be if when you walk in the door each night you have someone yelling 'Daddy!' as they leap into your arms?" Tim asks.

If you move your head to within an inch of the computer screen in your office, you'll see very little. Move back 10 feet and you'll see the whole picture, its context, and its relative importance. A problem that might seem to be the center of the universe is much reduced if you step back and take the broadest judgment on its significance.

Stress Buster #11: Make Time for Staff Socializing

Organize one day in the week when the company all meets together. If a company's staff is scattered throughout different locations, people might begin to feel isolated. Negative feelings—"I'm doing all the work around here"—can take root. One way to build camaraderie, Tim recommends, is to organize a weekly "watering hole" gathering, at 5 P.M. on a Friday, when the group gets together to unwind. Ask your workers what the funniest incident of the week was for them. Reward them with silly gifts. Get them to talk about their worst experience.

At Point B, all employees used to work at clients' sites and wouldn't see each other during the week until Friday's regular watering-hole meeting took place. "We'd do battle by ourselves all day long," says Tim, "but we needed a sense of shared purpose." These meetings became a place to cry, and later became informal discussion meetings on ways to push the business forward. "Retreat to your colleagues when you need to," Tim recommends.

Make a point to socialize with your employees on a regular basis. Ask individuals how they're doing, and tell anecdotes about your own naïveté and mistakes. Getting out among your employees and engaging them in conversation helps cut down on office politics, which is commonly caused by unspoken or unexpressed feelings of dissatisfaction on the part of a small minority of staff. Switch off your "boss persona" at lunchtime, and switch it back on again afterward. Get any employee anxieties out into the open, and they might quickly melt away.

Stress Buster #12: Create a Fun Environment in the Office

Serial Bootstrapper Donna Auguste, who started Freshwater Software in Boulder, Colorado, did not think glorious views of nearby mountains was sufficient for her staff. In keeping with the company name, every desk now has its own fish tank. In the doorway, a huge fish stands as the corporate icon, and the main meeting room has metal walls and bug-eyed windows to give the appearance of being submerged. Employees love the unique interior, and so do customers.

Xperts, an IT consulting business in Richmond, Virginia, provides a wide range of unusual benefits to its workforce. When employees need a car, Xperts provides a spare. A truck is also available—very handy for house moves. Also available on loan are laptops, projectors, a video-editing station, books, camcorders, and a CD burning unit.

Companies that pay attention to the comfort and needs of their employees have miniscule turnovers of staff. Employees are happy to go to work there, and the devil that is stress, is minimized.

Stress Buster #13: Never Take Things Personally

Relationships with customers and employees vary greatly, so don't interpret a setback as a personal attack. "If people decline to work for you," says Tim, "you can really feel it in the pit of your stomach. You feel they are attacking you personally, that you're a loser and that your business doesn't stand a chance." But Tim has learned to deal with such incidents without feeling personally attacked.

One way around taking setbacks personally is to get to know customers and employees as people. In the earliest days at Point B, the firm had an opportunity to work with Starbucks. "We had a phone call with the CIO of Starbucks," he recalls. "During the call she attacked my credibility and my competence, and I came out of it almost shaking." Tim felt bruised, but he managed to preserve a meeting he had arranged with her. His strategy was: "Get to know this person." He asked her about the pictures on the wall and the personal items on her desk. "A light switch turned on," Tim says, "and our relationship has flourished, even to this day."

It's easy to believe you're being victimized, or the world is against you. Think of it this way: If customers ignore your good advice and go in exactly the wrong direction, that's their problem, not yours. Conventional managers might not have the Bootstrapper's good sense of judgment. If you state and restate your opinion quietly and carefully, chances are they'll come back to you in the end.

If a customer finds it convenient to blame you, the supplier, for an error that was the customer's own mistake, you might have to live with it if it's a valuable contract. The customer's intention isn't nice, at the very least. It is, however, a good test of your ability to not to take it personally.

Stress Buster #14: Check Your Ego at the Door

Before you embarked on your career as a Bootstrapper, you might have come from a safe and secure job in the corporate world, perhaps a senior vice president in an important role. Customers treated you with respect and deference. They listened to your jokes. They paid homage to your business card. Now, as a Bootstrapper, your status might—at first—seem much diminished. Former clients won't return your calls anymore. You're no longer a big customer for the phone company. It might treat you differently, or rather indifferently. Tim warns: "Now you're not going to get all the smiles and firm handshakes you automatically got before." But don't worry—your day will come.

You might be the boss of your own business, but don't behave as if you're the CEO of a major corporation, and don't expect your employees to treat you like one, either. There is absolutely no need to get bent out of shape if you're not treated the same way you were when you held a big-shot job at a major company. This is Bootstrapping—it's not a rigid, formal hierarchy. Humility is the way forward. It helps you to stay driven.

Stress Buster #15: Make a To-Do List and Use the 80-20 Rule

By keeping a complete to-do list, you will have a better perspective of the work you need to accomplish. When you're juggling multiple tasks in your head they can seem overwhelming; just putting them on paper can make them seem more manageable. What feels like an endless list of things to do might boil down to just ten or twenty topics on paper.

Your to-do list allows you to prioritize the 20 percent that really matter so you can get the most out of your efforts. But tackling the remaining 80 percent can be satisfying, too. If your 80-percent list is long, concentrate on the clutch of small tasks that will take just a few minutes. Getting them out of the way will whittle down the list quickly and give you a feeling of accomplishment.

When you can dedicate quality time you should focus on the ugly 20 percent that will have the biggest impact on your business. When you have less quality time—at the end of the day when you're tired or while you're in an airport or on an airplane—you should focus on tasks that need to be done but are essentially "busywork," such as cleaning out your e-mail inbox or categorizing expenses.

Stress Buster #16: Upgrade Your Computer's Productivity

Maximizing your efficiency in all of those routine but essential PC tasks can, accumulatively, free up a lot of time for other activities. To begin with, handling e-mail efficiently can easily save you from 30 to 60 minutes a day. E-mail is easily the most common and effective communication tools, but allowing a buildup of 100 or 200 messages in your inbox is unmanageable. The sight of all those unanswered messages is a brute reminder of all your unfinished work. Aim to cut back your inbox to a maximum of twenty e-mails, so they're all are visible in the window, and you will sleep much better for it.

Here are two suggestions for keeping your e-mail under control: Keep your e-mail replies short—one or two sentences only, when possible—and learn your e-mail software's shortcuts. In many e-mail programs, for example, new contacts can be easily logged into your address book by clicking on the "name box" of the incoming e-mail. This is a quick way of logging in new people.

Stress Buster #17: Give Yourself a Mental Pat on the Back

You might have been in business for more than a decade, but stop for a moment and give yourself a round of "internal applause." What you've achieved is probably close to a miracle.

In 1988 Joseph Lahoud, a geologist, started LC Technologies, in Fairfax, Virginia, a business that built IT systems for, among others, the severely physically disabled. He and his partner, electrical engineer Dickson Cleveland, worked all hours to build the systems, and their clients came to organize their lives around LC's technology.

Joseph found that the toughest problems in running a business "was not the technology—it was financial management and marketing." He borrowed way above his income on credit cards, and refinanced his mortgage to help finance the business. His children's needs had to be paid for. His wife and his partner's wife worked largely unpaid in the business. The anxiety was enormous.

In 1990, making payroll became increasingly difficult. His staff thought they could see the end in sight. At a group meeting they said: "Joseph. You should close the business. Better if you didn't go any further." Joseph knew they were extremely loyal, committed, and dedicated people, and had his best interest at heart. But he thought: "We've come this far. Closing the doors would mean going back to an ordinary technology job and ending all we had achieved." The meeting ended in silence.

He and Dickson decided to continue working. But oddly, nobody left. Later one of them explained: "Joseph, we just couldn't bear the idea of leaving you both behind working there all alone. We couldn't abandon you like that. Actually, it made us find that extra energy to do all the things we knew we needed to do."

Gradually, more sales and development contracts came through and turnover rose to a steady $1.5 million a year. Later, the company hired a dedicated CEO, Shari Oley, an expert in marketing. By 2004, the business was stable—and Joseph and Dickson still owned 60 percent of the business between them. Surely it was time to give themselves one big pat on the back!

Stress Buster #18: Give Back to Those Less Fortunate

Not money. Give of your time! Giving money doesn't cut stress, and Bootstrappers don't have any money anyway. But if you're engaged in a caring activity of some kind—you'll feel better about who you are and what you're doing. "Nothing relieves stress better than taking care of others less fortunate than you," says Tim Jenkins. "Not only does it help keep your problems in perspective, it teaches you humility."

A group of Point B employees has been part of New Horizons, a group that serves breakfast to urban street youth once a month. They've been doing this as a team for over five years. "We set everything up, hand out the meals, and then take it all down again. The sessions were very stress relieving. We always clean up afterward, so each event had a great sense of closure," says

Tim. "It helps you forget about yourself; you realize that others have far greater problems than yourself."

a bootstrapping exercise

Review the stress-busting strategies in this chapter. Write down one or two things you can do in your own life and business to make the most of that strategy.

CHAPTER 12

HIRING THE RIGHT PEOPLE AT THE RIGHT TIME

"Look for the Three I's: intelligence, integrity, and initiative. You can't put in what God left out!"

—*Procter & Gamble hiring practice*

Whether you've started a hi-tech firm, a cleaning company, or a catering business, you'll continually be challenged to differentiate your business. How can the Bootstrapper make an instant impact? Answer: by the sheer quality and personality of his or her staff. If every time your customers pick up the phone, hear your employee, and smile and feel better, you're on the right track.

If you hire staff members who are intensely likable, your business will enjoy a far greater chance of success. A Bootstrapper can hire the smartest people, the know-it-alls, the sharp negotiators, the Mr. Smoothies, but if they're not likable, no one will want to do business with you. Never underestimate the human factor in business: First you build relationships, and then revenues.

a bootstrapper's tale:

Attracting the Best

oint B Solutions is a management consulting firm based in Seattle. It was started by "three guys, a laptop, and a letterhead," says cofounder Tim Jenkins. The trio wrote a check for $100 each, and since that day they have "never written a check back into the business."

Luckily, they had a client on day one, but from the beginning, the partners knew that the quality of their staff would be the overriding factor in any future success. Point B targeted midsize firms as clients rather than multinationals, and it offered its clients not large, unwieldy teams of workers, but just the project leaders.

But how could Point B attract management consultants from the big firms when it could offer almost none of the benefits? The answer was to create a business that was exceptionally "staff friendly." In a start-up, says Tim, "You have to differentiate yourself as an employer, too." The consulting business—where the routine conditions of long hours and lengthy periods away from home are notorious—demands a better way.

"First, we promised prospective employees that they would not be worked to the bone," Tim says. "Most important of all, we didn't just expect them to have other things in their lives, we *required* them to have them." This proved a big draw, and talented people were soon queuing up to join Point B to escape from the Big Five consultants.

Tim and his cofounders also pioneered a zero-hierarchy structure, and they created a company of peers. It was a flat hierarchy, which Tim calls "a recipe for chaos," but one where account managers were given maximum responsibility. This wasn't merely a gesture. "We granted our team leaders true authority," says Tim. "And we don't try to second-guess them. They take true ownership of their piece of the business. People come here because they are eager to build something."

Staff development was a critical factor in taking the business from a fledging consulting business to a thriving midsize firm. Instead of formulating a preconceived business strategy, the founders decided to let the staff build the firm on the opportunities that emerged through existing contracts. Today, the firm has thirty-five to forty account managers, whose roles have emerged through "organic job creation," says Tim.

Even more important, Point B's compensation scheme rewards contributions made by staff to the extent that individuals can double their salary through a special annual bonus provision. Those who have served a client particularly well, or creatively, or boosted the firm through sales, or who have helped recruit good people to Point B, are handsomely repaid.

Your First Hire

A business is created through the sheer will of the Bootstrapper. "Your first hire in sales is probably the single most important hire you'll ever make," says Brady Meltzer, RightNow sales manager. Don't hire the first or the tenth person who walks into your office. Hire only the Right Person—and this can take some time.

Making sales be your prime objective, a second salesperson (someone besides yourself) is likely to the Bootstrapper's first choice. But to start with, you might not need a star salesperson, or any star employees at all. There are always plenty of professional salespeople on the market, but remember, no salesperson, however professional, will be as passionate about your business as you are. This means you must be able to teach your sales force all of the steps that lead to making a sale.

"A Bootstrapper needs an active salesman who can later be turned into a trusted lieutenant," Brady adds. "Eventually this lieutenant will start hiring, too, so this initial employee must be first class. If you start with a weak foundation employee, you'll only get a weak sales force."

The first person you must employ is someone who can take the pressure off you, the Bootstrapper. This person is usually a salesperson.

What Type of Employees Do You Need Most?

The Bootstrapper needs a pool of loyal foot soldiers capable of physically making, assembling, dispatching, and monitoring delivery of the product or fulfilling the service. Competent, hardworking, task-oriented individuals are best. Look for "diamonds in the rough" as your first employees. Always give even the most unlikely individuals—the characters, the off-the-wall personalities, and mild eccentrics—the chance to prove themselves. You won't regret it.

One of the best-performing salespeople employed by RightNow Technologies in the early days was a man who was crazy about skiing. For the first two years he was the company's best-performing salesperson, even though he had no previous sales experience. He worked extremely hard—and efficiently—during the week, and disappeared into the mountains on weekends. In his soul, his job and office routine were merely methods of getting himself onto the slopes, and after two years he found a full-time job in the ski industry and waved goodbye to a promising sales career. We wished him well and thanked him for his contributions. Another jewel was a twenty-four-year-old woman who was then working as a nanny. She proved to be utterly tenacious and learned the business quickly.

Another type of character to look for is the jack-of-all-trades, who is happy doing a range of jobs. Susan Carstensen, a senior manager and one of RightNow's earliest employees, says: "You are looking for people who will roll up their sleeves, do multiple tasks, and above all, don't want to work in a silo."

As a start-up, you can't expect the best-qualified people to apply to work for your tiny little company. That's fine, because you rarely need them in the early days. Frequently, qualifications are irrelevant. Over time you'll observe that, from your pool of foot soldiers, a number of key talented individuals will emerge who will more than surpass your expectations. It is they who can be trained to become your first team leaders.

Where to Find Them

Recruitment firms can cost $10,000 to $15,000 per hire. That option is way beyond the reach of a Bootstrapper. So where can you find the best people? A Bootstrapper usually relies on a personal network of trusted colleagues, family, friends, and past contacts. Start by asking yourself a simple question: "Who are the most helpful people I know?" No, really, answer the question. Who are they? When you think about it you suddenly realize how few there are. But search for them anyway. In fact, you should be searching for them months and years before you launch your start-up. But if you start from this point, you are laying the firmest of foundations for your business—whether you realize it or not.

One of the most helpful people you know might be a library assistant who works at the library only on Saturdays. At the library she scurries about helping people all the time. She's forever unblocking the copier and never gets upset when a kid has only 45 cents for a 60-cent late-book fine. And she can always find the catalog entry for that must-have book for the persistent, gardening-mad reader who's always in there on a Saturday. (Of course, this person goes to the library only on Saturday because he knows no one else during the week will spend the time to help him.) And at the end of her shift, this assistant is still smiling at customers. Amazing! Would she be willing to work for you?

Another most helpful person might be a man who works at the local supermarket. He knows the names of dozens of his customers, and he remembers them week in and week out. It also seems that his enthusiasm and contribution are not appreciated by his work colleagues, who mostly stare glumly at nothing in particular. The question you should be asking when you see such a person is this: "Would he come and work for my new business?" This is Bootstrapping recruitment at its simplest.

Having thought about it for a while, you might have a better idea of who you should be asking to join your business, if not today then someday. You might actually have already met dozens of these human "diamonds" whose conduct and commitment have impressed you. Of course, many of these people might be complete strangers and they'd need to be properly checked out—but their attitudes speak volumes.

If the first few employees in your business are high quality, they can be good resources for quality staff members whom they've met in previous jobs, at college, or in their social networks. You won't need to spend thousands of dollars on recruitment agencies. Seek out people who are socially active and are embedded in the community and the local economy. People with a wide social circle are likely to be of much greater commercial use to your company than those who live relatively isolated lives.

Every year, thousands of college students are forced to undertake menial jobs in supermarkets and restaurants, just because they can't find better opportunities to use their brains and initiative. If you read the notice boards and call the career offices at local colleges, you'll be able to find many bright and energetic students. They will know lots of other smart and energetic people, too.

Mine your network and the networks of your friends, acquaintances, and neighbors. Spread your reach as wide as possible—to school, church, and sports clubs—wherever you have a personal connection.

When Should You Start Hiring?

For the Bootstrapper, the time to start hiring is when a critical moment has arrived—when you secure an order and understand what steps need to be taken to maintain your business. Begin by employing generalists—those who can undertake a broad range of tasks. As your business grows and those tasks become more specialized the Bootstrapper can go out and find dedicated specialists.

If your business employs just twenty people, the Bootstrapper can direct everybody's activities in the company easily enough.

a bootstrapper's tale:

"My name is Jennifer, and I'll be your first employee."

Lon McGowan was just twenty-two when he started his Seattle company that aimed to distribute $89 iClick digital cameras to the American consumer. Soon after starting the business he was beginning to feel a bit lonely, because his erstwhile partner had left to join a bank on a comfortable salary. He couldn't think of a single person from his university days who had the mental toughness and gutsy personality he wanted.

Lon ran a newspaper want ad that yielded 300 replies, complete with resumes, but not one of the applicants had the start-up experience or the enthusiasm he was seeking. He was disheartened. Around three times a week, however, he ate lunch at a local inexpensive restaurant. He ate alone but was always given great service by one of the younger waitresses named Jennifer. He thought that this waitress might just know of someone who might want to take the risk of joining his start-up. "Well, actually," Jennifer replied to Lon, "I'm looking for a real opportunity myself. I want to put my degree in international relations to good use."

So Lon found his first employee. To begin with, Jennifer agreed to work part-time, another benefit for the busy Bootstrapper. She came into his office between 8 A.M. and noon, and sometimes late in the afternoon, and still kept working in the restaurant. She was happy to work for rock-bottom wages at the outset. Soon Lon needed her full-time and offered her a position as the company's all-important logistics manager. Three years later, Jennifer is still a key member of the McGowan Technologies team.

With twenty to forty employees, responsibility is gradually pushed down, and staff members must be able to work alone. As your business grows, job roles tend to become much narrower, and the task-oriented generalists give way to self-directed specialists, or more highly trained people who take on specialized tasks in marketing and accounting. They will operate more independently and require less day-to-day direction from the Bootstrapper. So find your generalists first, and make sure they're generalists with masses of initiative.

Jon Nordmark, CEO of eBags.com, advises Bootstrappers to use what he calls "gated hiring." "Never hire faster than your revenues," he says, "but when revenues hit a certain target— then recruit."

Finding Specialist Staff

Specialist staff of the caliber you're seeking are often particularly difficult to find. This is why there are so many specialist recruiting firms charging high fees for the services of computer programmers, engineers, and other professionals. The Bootstrapper can't afford those high fees, so keep an open mind about where you might connect with the specialist types you need. They can often appear in the most unlikeliest of places. Most of us have an amazingly comprehensive network of social and business tentacles—and we rarely use it. The act of cherry-picking the best people is one of the finest skills a seasoned Bootstrapper can adopt.

Another benefit of hiring only the very best people is that these best people know others just like them. So start your own employee referral program—one that rewards employees who find other good ones—as early as possible. It will save you a fortune in time and fees, and will keep your company from falling into mediocrity.

The better the people you hire, the lower your staff turnover will be (more on that in a minute). In a tiny organization, the total cost of replacing staff is huge, and it leaves a huge hole in the team. If the person who departs has been a key member of the team, and has been in daily contact with important customers, vital relationships could be endangered.

When your business gains critical mass, you'll be able to formalize your selection process. But again, who do you select, and who do you avoid?

People to Avoid

Well-qualified and experienced people might apply for your jobs, but often they don't have the energy or the stamina for the two- or three-year journey of late nights and sheer hard work that starting and building a business entails.

What you certainly don't need are managers or general administrators. Useless bodies equal overhead, and your business can't afford them. Also, beware of people who have worked in big companies for long periods because they often find it impossible to leave behind the big-company benefits. Some of them assume "they know better" and can't adopt the ethos of the Bootstrapper or comprehend the advantages of doing things differently in the way you and other unconventional individuals do.

In interviews, be wary of big-company people who say, "I've always wanted to work in a small company but I do need a month off in the summer" or those who say, "I'm happy to settle for less, but you must match my existing salary." Such comments are red flags indicating these people clearly are not cut out to join a Bootstrapped company.

Even worse, people from big companies often have awful preconceived ideas about what things costs. They know about managing costs in a big business, and often expect the same standard in a small one. You shouldn't change your way of spending just to get an ex-big-company employee, or you'll lose your credibility with the rest of your employees. If they've shared a stapler for years and get modest wages, and you go out and buy lavish office furniture for a new employee, they'll wonder about your sudden change in values.

To get a better handle on how people view the cost of running a business, ask them how much they would pay to rent an office or to rent a photocopier. How much do 500 business cards cost? What is a reasonable amount to spend on taxis? The answers you get will tell you how realistic they are about working for a Bootstrapped company.

What applies to managers also applies to salespeople. Big-company salespeople are always cruising the job market, and many of them have exemplary sales records. But selling for a Bootstrapped company is a wholly different game.

In a Bootstrapped business, a salesperson must play many roles—pre-sales assistant, product manager who is the liaison between the engineers and the customer, and full-time salesperson. Every salesperson is a "one-man band." Always ask for references, but don't contact only the references offered you (they will inevitably be glowing recommendations from colleagues or even friends). Instead, phone the prospective employee's former employer and see if you can talk to his or her ex-boss. Phoning rather than asking for a written reference gets better results because people talk about things they wouldn't commit to paper.

Now you're clear about what you don't want, but what should you really be seeking?

Traits You Absolutely Need

Seek the right personality, first and foremost, before you search for skills. Search for evidence of initiative, integrity, and intelligence.

"People's characteristics are more important than skills," says Susan Carstensen of RightNow. "Find people with fire in their belly. People who are hungry for experience. By definition, the hungrier ones are less expensive, too," says Susan, who was employee number twenty-four at RightNow. The hardest part is combining experience with hunger because only a few people will have the stomach to start all over again. By probing into the motivations of prospective employees, the Bootstrapper can get a clear insight into the individual.

Above all, try to determine if the candidate is a team player. Ask whether he or she has taken part in team sports, which is a good indication not only of team spirit but also of a strongly competitive nature. People who play team sports know in their hearts that if they don't perform, they will have let down an entire squad. Also, team players live and breath a competitive spirit—which is exactly what you want. During the interview, try to pinpoint precisely where and how the candidate contributed positively and objectively in their previous jobs. And invariably, people do best at the things they most like to do. If you ask them this question, you'll then find out where they have been adding value to the process in their previous jobs. What is the number-one trait most sought after by experienced Bootstrappers? Passion.

The Interview Process

Interviewing is something of a black art, but the Bootstrapper must try to form an impression about the intentions and priorities of the person in front of you. Ask yourself: Where is the logic in this applicant's career path? Is the job we're offering a natural progression of his or her past job pattern, or is this applicant just looking for an income?

"Ask a lot of behavioral questions during interviews," says Brady Meltzer of RightNow. "These will elicit how they will operate as your employee. In sales, for example, ask the candidate how they would prepare for a presentation, or prepare for a site visit, how they would close a deal, or how they would handle a discovery prospect."

How applicants answer your questions tells you what they could contribute, and more revealing, what they could not. If, for example, the candidate says he or she would create a demo Web site to show the client, that's a plus. But if the candidate says: "I would get my sales engineer to create a demo Web site," the candidate's clearly unable or unwilling to do the basics herself. That's another red flag.

Next, ask yourself: Is this candidate passionate about joining us? Does the candidate have the necessary element of enthusiasm and sparkle? Many individuals are not mentally prepared for the battlefield of Bootstrapping, and you should cut them out early on.

If you still believe the candidate is a "runner," move to eliminate the "gold diggers." Begin by offering pay rates at or below the market rate. This will immediately discourage those who are seeking a big-company salary as a condition of employment.

It is important for candidates to assure themselves that they can cope financially with the low salary and long hours you'll be requiring from your employees. If it turns out they have kids who are about to go to college, your job may not the right one for them. When in doubt, ask the candidate this question: "What's the least amount you can live on?" and await the response.

Yes, these are tough questions. But if you want only lean-burning individuals on your team, you've got to eliminate the fat.

Ten Questions to Ask in Interviews

1. "What is your greatest strength and your greatest weakness?" Unexpectedly, most people give candid replies, and this helps you decide if their strengths outweigh their weaknesses.

2. "May I call your previous manager and also your references and ask them what your strengths and weaknesses are?"

3. "Are there any reasons why long hours in a Bootstrapped firm might not be possible for you?"

4. "Where do you see yourself in five years?"

5. "What ideas for future products or product improvements would you suggest for our company?"

6. "Why did you leave your last employer?"

7. "What did you leave behind that you feel is of lasting value to your employer?"

8. "Did your parents—or do any of your friends—run their own Bootstrapped business, and if so, do you think you've got a real grasp of what it takes to run a Bootstrapped business? Does that sort of challege appeal to you?"

9. "Did you take part in team sports in college/high school?"

10. "Why does our type of business appeal to you, and do you have contacts in our sector who might help our business? With your permission, may we speak to them?"

The Review Procedure

Oh no, it's not over yet. Not by a long stretch. Many ardent Bootstrappers take several more steps to sort the wheat from the chaff.

Put a prospective employee into a group of people—possibly over lunch—and watch his or her interaction closely. Does this person "belong"? Where would this person "fit"? Is there a big ego to contend with? The keenest Bootstrappers go to extreme lengths to make sure that their would-be employee is the right one. For one thing, employment decisions are often impossible to get right on the basis of an interview alone. Many of your candidates have been through dozens of interviews; they've become practiced and polished performers. But the Bootstrapper is not so easily persuaded.

Your next move is straightforward—test candidates out, one by one, on paid assignments, and now see how they perform. At RightNow Technologies, all prospective programming employees are given a paid project to undertake. The policy is called "try before you buy." Too often in the past, "perfect" candidates on paper underperformed by a wide margin in practice. On the basis of this paid project, a decision is made on whether a candidate should be hired. Out of 100 résumés received, about five candidates are selected, three are given projects, and about one is hired.

Training Key Sales Staff

Most conventional employers look for performance, not potential. They believe they have a right to demand experience and a healthy, relevant track record. As a Bootstrapper, you don't have that luxury. That means you will have to train your few hand-picked salespeople in depth. As a Bootstrapper you know how to sell, and if you're an ace Bootstrapper you'll be able to teach the art of selling above all other skills. Firing up your salespeople's potential and converting it into performance takes time—but every moment you can devote to this effort will not be wasted.

There's nothing like jumping into the deep end of the pool to train people quickly. Give your new salespeople a broad set of questions to ask. Get them to pitch to you over the phone as if you were a customer. Yes, really. Get them to call you from their office—to your office. Fire questions you know they can't answer, and see how they react. Sound short-tempered. Test their knowledge of the product and its advantages. What did they miss?

When you think your novice salesperson is ready, send him or her out for a day of making cold calls. Go along on the calls, sit quietly, and listen in on the conversation. Don't utter a word; just analyze each call with him or her afterward. What went wrong?

How could the conversation have progressed better? How did he or she get into that dead end? And, or course, what went right? It's surprising how quickly your protégé will learn enough of the rudiments to start bringing in some business.

Forging an Efficient Office Environment

In a young business, simple but essential competencies really matter. This might not be well understood, or it might be considered too obvious, but an inefficient office environment is a terrible and disheartening place to work in. And for those fast-moving, ambitious, impatient, quick-thinking employees you've recently taken on, it is simply intolerable.

In a Bootstrapping situation, it is vital that everyone is trained in basic tasks. These tasks include refilling the office printer with paper, replacing the ink cartridge, and answering the phones. Take, for example, the handling and redirection of internal calls. How often have you found that employees of companies you call don't know how to use the internal phone system? It's because they've never been taught. To an outsider the company looks hopeless. A degree of chaos is all part of the fun of working in a young, Bootstrapped company. But to outsiders, you should make every effort to appear to be a slick operation.

Every employee at your firm must be able to hold a confident conversation with anyone who calls your company; otherwise you will look amateurish at best, and incompetent at worst. Employees must know essential information, such as your zip code, fax number, and the mobile numbers for emergency callbacks.

Typically, in an office of ten people, around eight or nine could be on the phone at any one time. But when a call comes in—who answers it? It is essential that every employee, even the book-keeper, is fully aware of your product and all of its benefits, and can keep a high-value prospect engaged in informed conversation for a few moments until the right contact can take over the call. Don't forget—your company's reputation is on the line with every incoming call. A key prospect might be testing your reaction time anonymously. The caller might have been thinking: "Is this another small amateurish outfit wasting my time?" But your efficient, timely response will assure your prospect otherwise.

Again, it might sound simplistic, but unless these disciplines are maintained, your business will never run smoothly. Inevitably, the more competent staff spend much of their time dealing with the incompetencies of other lazy or untrained staff. It's surprising how often conflicts arise from this phenomenon. The time-consuming need to make up for the gaps in other employees' competencies is a consistent topic of gossip and raw irritation in many offices.

In an organized office, staff ought to know where individual employees are, and if someone is absent, when that person is due back in the office. An office might install a big readable noticeboard, where the movements of staff are up there for all to see immediately.

Make sure all your new recruits undergo an induction course that provides them with knowledge of the rudiments of your office life as early as possible. Collective competence often comes from working as a well-trained, well-drilled, and above all, coordinated team. If you don't achieve this, your best people with those bright, active minds will not stay for long.

Be Flexible

While some employees are extremely good and hardworking, the first job they are given might not suit them. It could be that they are excellent at building relationships with existing customers, but much less confident with cold-calling. So think again. What other job would be better for them, and for you? Match an emerging opportunity with the right internal employee wherever possible.

Hanging onto Your Staff

Once you've assembled this great staff, how do you keep it together? Personal gestures go a long way. Gifts, if sent soon after an accomplishment, are always well received. Every culture has its own code of gift giving and receiving. Too lavish and you risk making the recipient feel he or she is being "bought." Too little and you end up looking stingy. Staff anniversaries are important, too, and should be celebrated.

Amid the fire and fury of the long hours that everyone is putting into the business, take a moment to thank not just the employees but also the families for their sacrifice. Very often it is the families who bear the heaviest burden, especially if, for example, a salesperson on one of your key accounts isn't home three weeks out of four. Moreover, the act of thanking the families for their contribution goes down very well with employees—if only because as a corporate gesture it is still rare, and therefore all the more unexpected.

Whole-Company Meetings

Weeks come and weeks go, but often employees are cocooned in their own niches and lose touch with the rest of the company's activities. The Bootstrapper, who is also working hard, can lose day-to-day contact with staff, and staff members can lose contact with each other.

A way to prevent isolation, increase trust, and promote corporate loyalty is to organize regular "All Hands on Deck" meetings, when the staff is told about the latest ups and downs of the company's progress. Urgent problems with the company's financial health, strategy, and future prospects can also be aired. Equally, it's a perfect time for you to engage employees in discussions about the most pressing and irksome issues they might be facing—but you weren't aware of.

Don't assume the quiet ones aren't contributing. Often they are listening intently to all opinions, and then they come out with that "killer" solution to the problem, surprising everyone. In addition, if a staff member offers a solution that cannot work, don't allow anyone to criticize him or her. Praise that employee for the courage to suggest an unconventional solution, and ask the rest of the people for an unconventional idea that could work.

Encourage open-mindedness and frank discussion. Again, push your employees hard to think of interesting solutions and to express them out loud. One solution that might have failed with one particular customer could be ideal for another. Many "silly" ideas have saved the fortunes of companies in the past. Yours could be next. Examine all the possible solutions. Ultimately, the sum of ideas from everyone is much more powerful than the isolated thoughts of the few.

Without the meeting, however, there will be no cross-fertilization of ideas in your company. Such meetings can revive and maintain the enthusiasm and the spirit of community that the company first started out with. Preserve and cultivate your company team spirit.

Back Your Staff at Every Opportunity

Provide your employees with a "high-trust" work regime that gives them maximum scope for flexibility and initiative. Rob Irizarry of RightNow says, "If you must create a rulebook or a procedures book, keep it slim. You must allow the employee to bend the rules in the customer's benefit, when it is in your and the customer's best interest." Sales staff in particular must be sufficiently empowered with the authority to act as they think best.

All employees should be encouraged to grasp the initiative. Staff should be told: "Look around you. Do you see responsibility? If so, pick it up and run with it." If they see a roadblock? "Go over it, under it, or through it."

a bootstrapper's tale:

We Love It Here

During the tight job market in 1999, it was difficult to get first-rate people to consider working at RightNow Technologies' offices in Bozeman, Montana. Everyone wanted to be in Silicon Valley, in spite of the traffic and two-hour commutes. Or so it seemed. RightNow hit upon the idea of a special employment Web site, which has since become the main recruitment hub of the company. It's named *www.IloveItHere.com,* and it describes in detail Montana's pristine environment, good work-life balance, low property prices, and easy access to ski resorts and national parks—a big draw for many—and the ten-minute commute.

For programmers and engineers working in Silicon Valley, many of whom endure long traffic jams and ninety-minute commutes in each direction, the words on the Web site were enticing. When the site first appeared, it attracted more than 2,500 resumes, and by 2003 Right-Now had hired 120 new employees through the site. Even better, the Web site retains candidate resumes in its database, in case a job comes up in the future that fits the applicant's qualifications. By receiving applications directly, RightNow can avoid paying recruiter fees.

The Bootstrapper must be open to new ideas. If the boss likes innovation, it ensures that the whole organization is responsive and nimble. Be an optimist. Have a positive view of the business—and keep everything moving. Never stand still.

What Employees Want and Deserve

In survey after survey, employees want have pride in their company, an opportunity to learn and advance in their job, and a good work-life balance. Promoting your employees into to more senior positions creates a natural hierarchy that is more harmonious than if you recruited outside employees. New senior hires are often perceived as "having it easy" because they never experienced the tough early days. Some entrepreneurs find it difficult to take one step back and place their trust in their people. But if you do, they will become more dedicated to their work, and this will free you to concentrate on the more strategic business issues.

Fear not, multinationals were all young once. You might already have a partner, like Gates and Allen, founders of Microsoft, or Messrs. Hewlett and Packard. But it takes even more courage to start alone. Some entrepreneurs find it difficult to take one step back and place their trust in people. But if you do, your employees will become more wrapped up in their work, and this will free you to concentrate on the more strategic business issues.

And the first of these—once you've established a working business—is to ensure that your customers are receiving first-rate service, which is the subject of our next chapter.

a bootstrapping exercise

Go back to "Ten Questions to Ask in Interviews" in this chapter and create your own interview list of at least twenty questions.

CHAPTER 13

You Live or Die by
Your Customer Service

"The world cares very little about what a man or woman knows;

it is what the man or woman is able to do that counts."

—*Booker T. Washington*

With so much of the world becoming standardized and interchangeable, there is very little to differentiate your business from a legion of other companies. Except, that is, the special effort of backup support you provide to all your customers. In particular, this means the kind of service they *remember* you provided, which is the main reason they keep coming back to you for more products and services. A high level of customer service is still relatively rare in business—so this is one of the core ways a Bootstrapped business can stand out from the rest. Luckily for Bootstrappers everywhere, 98 percent of companies don't provide quality customer service to their clients. This is your opportunity.

Customer service is far more than just problem solving and "fire fighting." Rob Irizarry, RightNow Technologies head of customer service, is a passionate believer in the arts and practices of the craft. He says: "Customer service is too often seen as that 'red-headed stepchild' nobody wants." It's considered that infernal cost center that is truly costly. "I couldn't disagree more," Rob says. "Giving excellent service can turn your customer service unit into a key revenue center. No question about that." Not many companies have bothered to quantify the bottom-line impact of effective customer service, but they should, says Rob. "Do it once a year and you'll be pleased you did." In terms of sales opportunities, Rob doesn't need to be convinced. "Customer Services gives you endless opportunities to upsell, cross-sell, on-sell," he enthuses. "It can supply a host of leads that result in far greater dollar revenue. Above all, if it's done well, customer service retains customers year after year."

Customer service can also act as an efficient "intelligence service." This is because your customer service staff often hear things that customers would never tell your sales force. In many ways the relationship between your customers and your customer services staff can be much closer, more trusting, and less adversarial than their links to your sales team. Customer intelligence of this kind can often keep you aware of what's really going on inside a customer's business. It can provide early signals of new sales opportunities, or it can supply early warnings of trouble ahead. Forge your customer service department into both an "engine room," where it solves problems and keeps your business pushing forward on a daily basis, and a "crow's nest," where keen-eyed, perceptive representatives see far ahead, look out for the icebergs, and even provide a road map that drives the behavior—and the direction—of the whole company. Along with sales, customer service should be an effective part of a Bootstrapped organization.

Take one small example. A key ally of yours, a manager at a valued client, tells you he'll be leaving his company in four weeks.

That manager might not have told anyone at his company that he's leaving. But he trusts you enough to impart this crucial piece of information. Now you can track his departure, hopefully to a prime position at his new employer where he might buy your service again there, too. Concurrently, your customer services manager can monitor the arrival of the new manager who took your ally's old job. Your manager can check out this person's level of knowledge and affection toward your product or service. If the new person doesn't know much about it, a visit from one of your salespeople—with the objective of maintaining an existing customer and getting the new hire up to speed—might be key to keeping the business.

Going the Extra Step: Customer Education

At PrintingForLess.com, customer education, in addition to customer service, is crucial to the business. "One third of our customers are buying four-color printing for the first time," says CEO Andrew Field. "Most of our customers are other SMEs [small to midsize enterprises] which have no in-house graphics designer, nor do they employ a full-time print buyer, so our ability to explain things plainly and clearly is a key reason why they keep coming back."

If you manufacture a product, especially a consumer item, don't expect many customers to read the manual. Instead, they will call your customer service line and complain that this and that "doesn't work." Very often the feature is in perfect working order, but the ignorant customer is frustrated and needs someone to blame. This is where customer "education" is the prime element in your service.

a bootstrapper's tale:

A Pioneer of Great Service

If there were a first prize for being a veteran Bootstrapper, especially in the area of customer service, Les Schwab would be a worthy winner. Now in his eighties, he started Les Schwab Tires, a tire repair shop, in a shack in Prineville, Oregon, back in January 1952. Since then his business has become a byword for corporate excellence, open accounting, and unbeaten customer service.

Les's level of service is so legendary that generations of drivers who have gotten service at any one of his 330 shops across the western United States swear they will never go anywhere else for tires for the rest of their lives. Free flat-tire repairs for customers are just the beginning of the great service Les offers. As one of his customers, you're likely to get a wheel-clean even if you never asked for it. When mechanics change a tire, they clean the car afterward. They don't leave behind the collection of oily black finger marks you've come to expect after a visit to other repair shops. One long-standing customer said: "I thought this was some sort of a fluke. But my experience with them has taken me to a number of different stores over the years. It's become pretty obvious to me that their fixation on customer service is company wide."

On the corporate honesty scale, Les's company is at the opposite end from Enron. From the very beginning Les Schwab introduced an open-book policy for the company's accounts. Anyone can find out about the company's performance at any time. The current president of the company, Phil Wick, started as a lowly sales manager, underlining the company's practice of promoting from within. Schwab is now the largest independent retailer of tires in the United States. With little fanfare,

Les and his wife Dorothy have built a business that boasts $1.2 billion in annual sales. Far from living in the lap of luxury, Les still lives in a modest house and works part-time in the business. If a you're searching for a model of customer service, look no further than Les Schwab.

Building Loyalty Through Customer Service

Another way you can use customer service is to keep clients fully informed about your company's progress. "Tell all of your customers about your ups and downs," recommends Susan Carstensen of RightNow Technologies. "Make them part of your adventure. Enthuse them by asking them to become a participant in your way forward. Everyone likes to feel part of a success story." Your boundless enthusiasm will be infectious. It will breed a great deal of loyalty among your clients.

Don't forget, a customer relationship is the most organic and highly sensitive of entities. "A customer is only as good as your last interaction," says Brady Meltzer, RightNow's sales chief. "That interaction could be many things—a Webinar, your last phone conversation, or it could be the time your customer at the airport bumped into RightNow's janitor, because he was wearing a company T-shirt."

From the data collected by your customer service unit, search high and low for those top "reference-able" customers you can use as shining beacons of success in your future marketing. Some of the best ones might have used your product for years, and they're still good customers, in part, because of the good relationship your customer service people deliver.

In short, customer service is the number-one storehouse of customer relationships—and it should be treated as nothing less than a treasure store.

Twelve Ways a Bootstrapper Can Keep Customers Happy

#1: Tackle Problems Very Quickly
"It's a lot easier to put out a small fire than to tackle a blaze," says Rob Irizarry. When a problem arises, call back *immediately*.

Find out what went wrong, and go fix it. Calling back early can often stun a complaining customer. A dissatisfied customer might send you an e-mail saying he's very unhappy with one aspect of your product. He'll assume you'll just read and ditch it. Oh, no you haven't. Call him back within minutes, and politely confront the issue head-on. Your customer will be astonished by the speed of your reaction. Never leave problems to fester, or your customer will sneer to colleagues: "Well, we told them—but they never bothered to come back to us." Think about it: If you sit down in a restaurant and nobody comes to serve to you—how long do you wait before you leave? Five minutes, ten at the outside? And would you ever return?

When a customer complains, and it's your fault, just let the customer 'vent'—don't try to find a logical path to solve the solve the problem right away. First, go into "grief counseling" mode. Be understanding, and express your sympathy with the customer's problem. When you've got the customer off the ledge, you can start to talk through the steps to a solution. "First let them feel they're being heard—not just listened to," Rob points out.

#2: Keep Your Word

If you promise something to a customer, don't fail to deliver. Why? Because you and your company must stand by your stated objectives in order to be taken seriously. This is not mere posturing and the empty exclamation of lofty principle, says Rob Irizarry. "You've got to have something you stand for," he says, "and then do it unfailingly." No recipient of this level of service will forget it. "There's always time to do the right thing," he adds. Always underpromise and overdeliver. This avoids the danger of failing to keep your word. If you need time to find a solution, say so. This will give you breathing space in which to "noodle," or think over the conundrum. If you continue this strategy, customers will soon recognize that the quality of your word is as good as your products. And customer service is where they'll find that first. Customers are buying a relationship from you in addition to your product.

#3: Ignore the 2 to 3 Percent of Humanity Who Are Simply Impossible

"They were born unhappy and they will die unhappy. Nothing you will do will change that," says Rob. Some serious management studies in the United States have shown that certain people are die-hard, incorrigible complainers, who will never be satisfied with the level of service you provide. Spot these Mr. Miseries early in your business and avoid them like the plague! They often crop up because other companies have learned to avoid them, too. Instead, put your efforts into customers who matter, and those who appreciate your efforts on their behalf.

#4: Ingrain the Process of Listening to Customers from Day One

Most of us are much happier talking rather than listening. In a Bootstrapped business that is utterly dependent on the wishes of its customers—the act of listening must take precedence. Few of your staff will comprehend how important this is. You do. And it is your duty to teach them early that listening to the customer is critical. Insist upon it. The Bootstrapper must formalize this process when he or she starts the company. Once you have this principle firmly in place, your company is on the right road. The intelligence and insights your customers tell you will make or break your company's fortunes.

#5: Become a Trusted Adviser and Provide Proactive Service

When a problem occurs, do whatever it takes to solve it. Try to discern what the real issue might be. This will happen only if you listen carefully. The customer might be complaining that the flash on his newly bought camera doesn't work—but that might not be the real issue. Dig deep enough to learn what the problem is; don't just treat the symptom.

Call valued customers automatically at set intervals. Give them a "Time to change your oil" call. Don't just ask: "How are things going?" Instead, research their corporate health before-hand if possible. Say: "I noticed traffic had fallen on your site. Is there anything I can do to fix it?"

#6: Learn to Manage Expectations

A Bootstrapper will do everything to make his or her first clutch of customers happy, including providing customer service on call 24/7, regardless of the personal cost. But once you start to get dozens or hundreds of customers, your earliest customers must accept that they can't expect to continue getting that level of service, or at least not for free. When the time comes, adjust their expectations with a mixture of charm and firmness, and ask them to start paying for a "Rent a Human" level of support.

#7: Set Up a Survey to Monitor Customer Satisfaction

Measure customer satisfaction on a scale of one to five, and don't ignore the resulting report. Read it and absorb the lessons, especially the hard lessons it will inevitably teach you. If any customer rates your quality of service below "satisfied," then do something about it. Find out what the cause of dissatisfaction has been, and act to restore the goodwill. Sending an e-mail is not good enough—only firm corrective action will succeed in solving the problem. Conversely, it helps to know exactly who your happiest clients are, too, because happy customers buy things!

#8: Acknowledge Feedback

There will be hitches and glitches in any new product. Reward your key customers with a bottle of champagne if they find something wrong that leads to a major improvement in your product. Since eBags started in 1999, it has received from its customers an astonishing 336,000 product review submissions, many of which are posted on its Web site. Now the company lives and thrives by the volume and detail of this independent customer input. "Customer testimonials are absolutely vital," says CEO Jon Nordmark. "New customers buy a new bag almost exclusively on the basis of other customers' experiences and preferences. They particularly like the good points mentioned, and very often don't seem to care about the bad features."

#9: Monitor Your Customer's Use of Your Product

If your customers are not using your product much—find out why. This is serious. Either the product isn't appropriate for their needs or they don't know how to use it properly. They might be too embarrassed to tell you. Explore further. Alternatively, find out if they are using it in a novel way you'd never expected. Find out more and see if you can upgrade your product in any way to perform this new task.

#10: Ask Your Customers for "Love Letters"

Few customers will tell you how fabulous a job you are doing on their own. You'll have to ask them to write down what they like about doing business with you. As your customers begin to list the benefits, your customers will inevitably discover benefits they hadn't appreciated before, and will be astonished at your product's usefulness. They'll appreciate your business even more. Also, ask your customers to quantify, if they can, what your product has done for their bottom line. This is priceless intelligence. When your customers' praises—or "Love Letters" as they're called in the trade—arrive, utilize them for maximum marketing effect.

#11: Treasure Your Earliest Customers

It is vital that you not forget those early customers who purchased your product when you desperately needed their business. They saved you from extinction, so don't ignore their needs even if you've got much larger customers today. Keep your early customers happy, too. Brady Meltzer of RightNow says: "Those early customers who bought your product for $500—not the $5,000 you might now be charging—took a big risk with you. Remember: The guy who's going to be with you longest is the most important customer of all."

#12: Inaugurate a Regular Customer Event

Your first event could be a breakfast, a dinner, or a simple barbeque at your house with a dozen customers. But in time the customer event could grow to become a full-blown, fully comprehensive user conference.

The User Conference

If handled properly, a user conference can be hugely rewarding to your company and to your staff, too. Don't forget that many of your support staff might never have met their contacts at client firms, even though they might have talked to the clients almost every day for years. When RightNow started its first user conference six years ago, just five customers attended. But that didn't matter. The five had a great time, and strong relationships were forged with RightNow staff. In the second year, thirty-five customers attended, and eventually more than 300 showed up.

Your user conference doesn't need to be expensive. In fact it should never be lavish, but it must be welcoming. There should be lots of social networking interspersed with enlightening, right-on-point seminars on your latest offerings. Always insist that your "engine room" people attend the event. If you are a catering firm, don't leave the cooks and the chef at home. If you're a software company, make sure the development team shows up. Many of your customers will be highly knowledgeable about software, and will want to interact with key software engineers at length.

"What? Let software engineers meet the customers?" I hear you say. Yes, really. There might be a culture clash to begin with, but a rapport will develop quickly. Both sides will learn an awful lot from the exchanges. Break down barriers whenever you can. If you believe any of your engineers will have difficulty speaking to customers, help them out—see if you can find a program for them that teaches human interaction skills.

Now Count the Benefits

First of all, your company receives "wonderful" feedback. It's free, it's direct from the horse's mouth, and it'll contain a large number of product ideas and improvements you'd never have thought of. Second, customers are delighted to be able to talk directly to the people "who make things happen." Personal links are forged that can last for years, even decades. The human contact element is essential. Meeting a contact face-to-face, even for a few moments, is worth a year's interaction on the phone, and probably much more via e-mail. The bottom-line benefits of a well-run user meeting are immense—and they often endure for an extended period of time. For twelve months to be precise—when the next one happens.

"Please Meet Our Other Customers"

Another benefit of the user conference is that customers love talking to other customers. All are members of the same fellowship—your most prized set of clients. They'll compare notes, exchange war stories about their businesses, and best of all, they'll chat about the different ways in which they've applied your products.

Establish an "Ask the Expert" room at the event, and run it 24/7 (well, almost). This gives shy clients, those who are sensitive about expressing their ignorance, the unique opportunity of meeting with one of your specialists one-on-one. At RightNow's events, programmers are ready and waiting to walk customers through novel features, answer questions about existing products from puzzled users, and inch through complicated sequences of IT activities step-by-step, on a one to one basis. Customers love this sort of attention.

Over the months, many customers build up a veritable mountain of questions. By providing an "Ask the Expert" room, they can obtain instant solutions. "Call it the 'One & Done' process," says Rob Irizarry. "And [the customer] won't feel embarrassed to call up your expert because he knows him already. And he knows his call will be welcomed. That's just as important," Rob points out. At a user conference, being able to talk to the experts is by far the best way customers can interact with your staff.

"Prospects, Please Meet Our Satisfied Customers"

Who could be better salespeople than your own customers at your user conference? A user event of any kind, large or small, is an unrivaled opportunity to introduce your latest crop of prospective customers to the opinions, experiences, and pure satisfaction of your existing customers. The latter will give glowing endorsements of your products and services. If they didn't like your offerings, they wouldn't be there. So invite as many hot prospects as you can to your customer events. Eventually, many customers will start to attend your conference not merely to find out more about your products, but to discover how you've built such an effective and successful corporate culture.

a bootstrapper's tale:

The Dog Ate My Camera

Lon McGowan, founder of iClick, the digital camera supplier in Seattle, says, "Our company philosophy hinges on customer service." He declares, "No telephone menus, no voice mail boxes, just people [in order to cater to] the important and time sensitive needs of our clientele. Our core competitive angle is to offer human customer support." According to Lon, only 5 percent of all camera sales result in a phone call, but 90 percent of queries are resolved with a single call. Customer education is also significant at iClick. Many queries don't concern the camera but issues such as PC compatibility. Would Lon consider outsource customer support to the Far East? "No way," he says. "Direct contact brings us great loyalty. They bought the product from us partly out of personal loyalty to our company—we are very grateful for that."

Lon has found that the difficult customer must have "his moment." One customer said that a dog had chewed his camera. Surprised that it wasn't working anymore, he demanded a replacement. Lon asked to see the original, and sure enough it was indeed covered in ferocious teeth marks, and smelled distinctly of dog. "We sent him a new one in honor of his dog's destructive prowess," says Lon. "The original now sits on my desk as a monument to customer expectations of our cameras."

iClick makes every effort to build enduring relationships with its camera-wielding buyers. Photos taken by iClick enthusiasts in places such as Croatia, the Philippines, Rome, and Paris have been given a special area on the company Web site. The innovation helps sales. Would-be customers can view the photos and reassure themselves that the picture quality of the iClick camera is equal to that of mainstream manufacturers.

The Rules for Quality Customer Service

Starting up and maintaining a good relationship with customers can be a difficult task, but once you get the basics right, good relationships can make the difference between the success and failure of your business. Always remember that your reputation is at risk once a customer loses faith in your service, because you'll have a difficult time restoring it.

Here are the rules to follow when dealing with customers:

1. Be honest. The number-one rule is to not make promises to customers unless you know you can deliver on them. And if problems arise and you can't solve them immediately, say so. Customers tend to be more forgiving if you level with them.

2. Don't give customers the runaround when they try to get a problem resolved. Deal with the problem as soon as it comes up, and ensure that it's resolved speedily, with the least amount of hassle to the customer.

3. Be friendly and polite in your dealings with customers. Ensure that they feel valued by your business and that their complaints or views are genuinely taken into consideration. In a telephone call, give customers a chance to air their grievances rather than you talking over them. Courtesy costs nothing and will go a long way to building a sound and long-term relationship with customers.

4. Focus on the objective. The primary objective of your customer service is to resolve problems, answer inquiries, and generally make the customer's experience of buying from you as pleasant as possible. Second, a customer service call is also a chance to sell your product, but do that sparingly and sensitively, because customers don't appreciate a hard sell if they need you to solve a problem.

5. Know your stuff. Dealing with customer inquiries requires knowledge of the business, the products and services, the prices, the terms and conditions, the guarantee terms, promotions, and so on. It's imperative that the people answering the inquiries know every aspect of the company and the product range; otherwise they will sound unprofessional and appear ill informed.

6. Use your customer service to help you refine your service or product. For example, if customers regularly call to ask questions about the assembly instructions you provide with a certain product, you should take this as a signal that the instructions are not adequately detailed or clear for all of your customers. This gives you the opportunity to provide better instructions next time, improving the customer experience as you go along, and reducing the number of calls you receive on that particular aspect of the service.

7. Keep your cool. There's no point in getting into a heated argument with your customers. Never lose your temper and always concentrate on the resolution rather than arguing over the details or who's at fault. Sometimes you might need to swallow your pride to retain the loyalty of your customers even when you know they are in the wrong.

8. Make it easy for customers to get in touch with you. Find out the most convenient ways for your customers to contact you. For example, if you run an Internet-ordering company, you might find that the vast majority of your customers prefer contact by e-mail. Therefore, you should ensure that you have a "contact us" link on every page of the Web site and in a prominent position. If you run a mail order company, your customers might prefer to contact you by mail or by telephone. Ensure that your contact details are on all your correspondence with customers—invoices, receipts, guarantees, compliments slips, letters, quotations, and so on—and that inquiries are answered promptly.

9. Don't use jargon or try to blind your customers with science. You know more about your product than your customers do, so you should seek to simplify and explain what's happening in plain, clear language. If the customer feels patronized or talked down to, he or she will be much less likely to buy from you in the future.

10. Try to structure calls from customers as best you can. If customers call with a grievance, allow them to air it. Once this is done, an experienced customer service rep will seize control of the conversation and direct it toward solving the problem. You should break the problem down into specific points to clarify the exact nature of the complaint and to show that you are aware of what the problems are. Go through the points one by one and offer resolutions there and then. Be clear about what the caller needs to do and what you have promised to do. Make sure the caller can reach you again if necessary or, if it's likely someone else might get the call, that individual will be aware of the nature of the original call.

a bootstrapping exercise

Think of the last three times you contacted a company's customer service department. Write down your experiences, and consider how your complaint or question could have been better handled.

Then write out a list of the areas of your future business most vulnerable to error or inconsistency, and therefore most likely to become the main focus of complaints to your customer service department. For each, think of a way to limit complaints and increase customer satisfaction.

CHAPTER **14**

ACT LIKE A WINNER

"Anything worth doing is worth doing well."

—*Philip Stanhope*

O ne of the biggest challenges facing a Bootstrapper is how to gain credibility with prospective customers. At first you don't have much to offer. Ultimately as you gain customers they can act as references for other customers. But how can you get those first few critical first reference customers? Here are some ideas:

1. Align yourself in some way with an established, noncompetitive company that has existing relationships with the prospective customers you want to sell to. Some aspect of your solutions might well be beneficial to them.

2. Offer a money-back guarantee. One way to reduce purchasing objections is to remove risk for the buyer. Your assurance, "If our product or service does not do what we say it will, you owe

205

us nothing," will make it hard for customers who have a real need to say "No."

3. Give your product or service to a few customers for a limited time in exchange for their agreeing to be references for other prospective customers later on.

4. Solicit influential people in your community or industry for their endorsement in the form of an article or quote. Send a product sample to a key journalist. Even one article in a reputable magazine could give you credibility and has the added benefit that it might generate some sales leads.

5. Solicit letters of endorsement from former bosses or organizations you have worked with in the past. For example, a letter from a former boss stating that he or she worked with you for five years and always found you diligent and honest could make the difference in getting that first client.

All these strategies center on leveraging other people's credibility. Use your imagination and you can certainly think of many other methods to gain credibility and get those initial customers.

How to Compete Against Larger, Better-Funded Competition

In 500 B.C., Sun Tzu wrote an extraordinarily insightful book on successful battle tactics entitled *The Art of War*. Business is very much like waging war and much can be learned from Sun Tzu. Some of the most useful concepts for the Bootstrapper are:

1. Know yourself and know your enemy, and few battles will be lost. Few things can replace preparation. The more time you invest in understanding your potential clients and their alternatives, the better prepared you will be. Surprises in sales calls are mostly due to lack of preparation.

2. Attack where the enemy is weakest. Don't attack your competition's strong points; instead, find the weak spots. If in your research you find that the competition is doing a good job servicing one aspect of your prospect's business, stay away from that point. Find where the competition is failing to satisfy their customers, and concentrate your energies there. You will gain much better results because the prospective customer has a reason to use your product or service.

3. Fight from positions of strength. Understand what makes your product or service better than anyone else's. Find prospective customers to whom your unique differentiation matters. Sell to those prospects. If your strength does not matter to the client, you gain no advantage.

4. Don't take ground you can't hold. In business that means don't sell a product or service you can't deliver profitably. It makes no sense to sell below your cost and then attempt to make it up on volume. The math just doesn't work, yet many businesses try to do it. Avoid this trap. As a Bootstrapper you will often be offered the contracts that nobody else wants. Be wary of taking such business.

5. Weigh the situation, then move. Or, to put it another way, "when in doubt, act." Often just doing the next thing will make your continued steps clear. Inaction is the enemy of any business and especially a Bootstrapped business. Fortunately you don't have enough money to make any fatal mistakes.

Preparation

As Sun Tzu knew, being prepared for battle is essential. The more you know about your prospective customer's business, your prospect's points of pain, your competition, the personalities involved, and anything else that might influence the ultimate purchase decision, the better your position to win. Spend the necessary time to find out about your prospective customers.

If they are public, read their annual reports and most recent quarterly filings. Review their Web sites. Call and inquire about their products or services. Locate some of their customers and talk to them.

If you've been dealing with a low-level individual and the time has come to meet with an executive, find out all you can beforehand. Ask your contact what the executive's "hot buttons" are. Find out what the company's major initiatives are for the year—if you can relate the value of your product or service to the company's major initiatives, you're in a better position to win.

Why would someone be willing to answer all the questions? Because answering your questions is in that person's best interests. In the end that person is trying to solve a business problem, and the more he or she feels you understand, the more confidence that person will have in your ability to truly help.

You need to turn over every rock looking for information, and then formulate a plan of attack based on your known strengths and your competitors' weaknesses.

Expect to Win

Once you have your game plan together, you need to expect to win. Your attitude is transmitted every time you speak to someone on the phone and every time you meet with someone. You need to expect to win in every sales situation. Expecting not to win will broadcast your doubts as if you were shouting "failure!" from the rooftops.

Would you be convinced by a sales representative who said this: "I'm not sure we can do what you want. We've never done it for anyone else, but I'm willing to give it a try. May I have your order today?" That sounds ridiculous; however, that's exactly what you're saying to a prospective customer when you don't expect to get the order. You must broadcast confidence, not arrogance, in your ability to meet customers' stated needs.

It's much better to say: "I've poured over your requirements and know without a doubt that we're going to be able to deliver. You'll be thrilled with the result. May we get started today?" To say it again: Expect to win.

How to Communicate Value and Be Paid Accordingly

In business-to-business transactions, companies need to calculate a return on investment (ROI). Understanding how companies calculate ROI can help in presenting your solution to them and will allow them to justify their purchase of your product or service.

You must remember that companies do not purchase products or services because they like the features or the color of the packaging. They buy them because they believe, or have been convinced, that the product or service will have tangible impact on their business. That's how companies figure out ROI. There are great books that have been written on value-based selling or solution selling. Buy one, study it and then apply it in your business-to-business selling efforts. The following is a brief introduction to value-based selling.

There are only two places to find ROI in a business: Your product or service either reduces your prospective customer's expenses or increases its revenue. This is where value lives—on the income statement. You are either increasing the top line (increasing revenue) or fattening the bottom line (reducing expenses). Other forms of business benefits end up impacting one of these two items. For example, if you manufacture a product that increases the quality of a product produced by your customer, then the impact of your product will be increased customer satisfaction, which translates into happier customers, which translates into more repeat orders and referrals, which translates into increased revenue. If your product allows your customers to improve the output of their manufacturing process, but has no noticeable impact on the actual product produced, then your impact is solely in reducing the costs of their manufacturing process.

One of your goals with early customers is to understand what business value your product or service creates for your customers—in rock-bottom tangible dollars. For example, if you can get an early customer to document that your product or service helped save the company $20,000 in costs in a single year, that provides an awesome selling tool for you to use with any other company similar to the one with the savings. Rather than saying: "I have a product that does X, Y, and Z," you can state with conviction: "We saved ABC Corporation over $20,000 in the first year because it used our product, and I'm sure we can do the same for your firm." Now that's a far more compelling proposition to put to a prospective customer. And if the example of savings is from one of the prospect's direct competitors, how can the prospect not look at your product or service?

So the first step is to figure out what sort of value your product or service creates for the prospective customer. It's either expense reduction or increased revenue, or both. The best way to do this is to talk to prospective customers and existing customers. In exchange for early use of your new product or service, for instance, you can get your first few customers to agree to work with you in order to document their savings or rises in revenue.

The savings or revenue increase sets an upper ceiling on the price you can charge your prospective customer. So, if your product or service costs more for you to produce than the savings or revenue increase you generate, go away and find another idea or another way of stamping down on your own costs.

But once you have the documented ROI—and a customer reference to prove it—you have an unbeatable sales weapon, something of awesome power in the market.

Measure Everything That Is Important

It is possible to drive a car without a gas gauge and a speedometer, but having them does help you assess when you're going to run out of gas or get a speeding ticket. In the same way, having good measures is essential as your business starts to take off. Not monitoring key business measures is a quick route to an empty gas tank. However, it's important that you measure only what is really important. Excessive complication or complexity in your business will add unnecessary overhead, clutter your dashboard, and hide the important trees in the forest. Find the essential few things you need to monitor and then develop policies to ensure you see them often.

As we discussed in Chapter 6, the first measure a Bootstrapper needs is a way to monitor cash levels and projections, and we used the cash flow forecast statement to do this. There are other critical indicators in your business as well. For example, if you are starting a business that manufactures products, you must track your inventory of completed products and raw materials. Too much inventory and your precious cash is tied up in illiquid form. Too little inventory and you can't fulfill orders. Either one can mean death. Or, if you are running a consulting business your backlog of work is essential. If you consume your backlog you will have expensive consultants sitting idle. It's important that you think about your business and determine what are the few essential measures you need to monitor.

Build a Solid Foundation

Growing a business is like climbing a ladder. Make sure you are firmly on the next rung before you reach higher; otherwise you might fall. Likewise in business, don't expand too quickly; your resources will get spread too thin and you might fall.

At RightNow Technologies growth exploded from the beginning. Revenue and the number of employees doubled every ninety days for two years. Resources became thinly spread. It was hard to get everyone trained. It was hard to maintain quality of service. Also, with half the employees starting new every ninety days, it was hard to maintain the culture that the company was based on. People bring with them prejudices and biases from previous work experiences. With so much influence from outside it was hard to plant in people the unique Bootstrapping culture of RightNow Technologies fast enough. Fortunately, the market slowed and hiring slowed, too, and this gave everyone a chance to catch their breath. A good analogy for this process is one from construction: You need to allow the foundation of a building to harden before you put the higher floors on top of it.

During the fast-paced early stages of a Bootstrapping enterprise, staff might feel as if they're driving a bus down a highway, leaning out the window, and trying to change a flat tire, all while moving at 60 mph. No one can keep up that kind of urgency forever. As you consider your next move, make sure your foundation is solid and if it is, you will have sound construction.

From "Bootstrapper" to "Leader"

A transition occurs in every growing Bootstrapped business. As the company gains mass and strength, the Bootstrapper can no longer make every decision or direct everyone in person. When does this occur? Usually after you've hired around twenty to thirty employees. This is also when the generalist multitaskers you hire early on start to become disgruntled. Why? Because their jobs are becoming more specialized.

This maturing of a business can be extremely unpleasant for the more ambitious type of Bootstrapper, especially one whose business is growing rapidly both in size and in sophistication.

The people you will need to let go are—invariably—your friends. Yes, you've worked with them for years. Achingly, they helped you grow the business. But, they are not happy *and* they are standing in the way of business growth. This maturation process is common to businesses everywhere. If you are successful, you will face it, too, but nothing will prepare you for it. How you handle change of this sort will determine whether your company can continue to grow.

The Bootstrapper must also change. He or she must transform into a Leader. Gone will be the days when you can make every decision. You must learn to trust others, not just with execution, but with the development of strategy. This is really hard, and for many entrepreneurs nearly impossible. Again, the experts advise: "Now that you have proven there is a market, you need 'professional' managers to help you." And in some aspects they are right, but be careful. Remember, you are still in charge and these "professional" managers work for you. Give them clear direction and define the boundaries of the sandbox they must play in. For example, be clear about how much money they have to do their job and the results you expect. If they push back, hear them out and if you agree, fine. Find a way to get them the resources they need or compromise with them. But, again, be careful! Just because XYZ MegaCorp used $1 million to launch a new product doesn't mean you need to. (You could avoid some of this confrontation if you question your applicants during the hiring interview process about their attitudes toward spending company money.)

The last thing you want to do is lose your Bootstrapping quality, that essentially pragmatic, "scrappy" sort of dynamism. If you do hire "professional managers," you will need to spend time training them on the ways of a Bootstrapper and deprogramming their tendencies toward corporate excess. You should never lose the scrappy, penny-pinching attitude, but you will need to cede some responsibility if you're going to keep your best staff.

Lastly, becoming a Leader helps your company develop credibility—a key asset in the world of business.

Innovation Is Not an Accident

Innovation is critical to the continued growth of any organization, and it is a deliberate act. Innovation allowed you to find that initial idea that launched your business. Look ahead and find ways to repeatedly develop innovations that will perpetuate and renew your business.

The Bootstrapper's mantra—"There is *always* another way"—leads to innovations because the Bootstrapper thinks hard about finding less obvious solutions to business problems. Open up the discussion and tell employees: "We need ideas, the best ones." Ask them to put their heads in their hands for ten minutes to think about the problem over the weekend. Deadlines propel innovation into the open because they force everyone to think hard. By thinking hard, by not giving up, by seeking imaginative solutions, the winning moves emerge.

As a Bootstrapper you must be ready to recognize and capitalize on the best ideas. Innovation is a deliberate act and you must explicitly cultivate it or it will not grow. Always remember: The Bootstrapping principles you use to start your business—innovative thinking, thrift, adaptability, and more—are the same ones you need to ensure that your business will endure and thrive for years to come.

a bootstrapping exercise

Following the Sun Tzu principles described in this chapter, evaluate and suggest changes to your current business plan.

APPENDIX

THE BOOTSTRAPPER'S
TOOLBOX

The following sections contain tools helpful for getting started, developing professional skills, and testing your own aptitude as a potential Bootstrapper.

Your "Getting Started" Checklist

The following is a checklist of things to consider in starting a new Bootstrapped business. Follow them and you will be on your way. Ignore them at your own peril!

1. Decide what you're selling and to whom. Outline the key features and benefits of your product or service on a single sheet of paper.

2. Identify potential customers and how to contact them.

3. Contact potential customers and start asking for orders. Of course, don't mislead customers about a service or a product that is not yet available, but don't let that stop you from asking for their business.

4. If your potential customers are not willing to buy—the most likely initial outcome—find out why. Take that information and update your product or service description. Return to Steps 2 and 3, until you believe you have the right idea.

5. Work out what product or service features have the best value proposition that you can deliver initially with your limited resources. Try to identify the minimal set of features or capabilities that will allow you to get your first customers. Make those features or capabilities your first product or service. You can always add more once the revenue stream has started.

6. When you have prospects willing to spend money, start making and delivering your product or service. Be careful not to spend more time than absolutely necessary. Your primary time and effort should still be devoted to selling. Try to get these initial customers to pay all or part in advance.

7. Grow your business incrementally. Add phones, workspace, and employees only when necessary and only when you already have the money. Concentrate on sales.

8. When sales take off, pull out the sledgehammer. Hire more salespeople.

9. Always remember to celebrate your successes.

The Bootstrapper's Reading List

As a Bootstrapper, you will need to continually develop your professional skills. The following books will help. Each covers an essential skill you'll need to develop as you grow your business.

Bottom-Up Marketing by Al Reis and Jack Trout (Plume, 1990)
The fathers of modern marketing discuss how to build successful strategies from tactics that work. This is required reading for Bootstrappers.

Business by the Book by Larry Burkett (Thomas Nelson, 1990)
The Good Book, that is. Biblical concepts applied to business management. If you endeavor to run an ethical business that is built on a solid moral foundation, this book will help.

The Fall of Advertising and the Rise of PR by Al Reis and Laura Reis (HarperBusiness, 2004)
A fascinating discussion on the value of (or lack thereof) of advertising. Read this book before you spend any money on advertising.

Innovation and Entrepreneurship by Peter Drucker (HarperCollins, 1985)
A classic text from the Father of Modern Management. A must-read.

The One Minute Manager by Kenneth Blanchard and Spencer Johnson (William Morrow, 1982)
The best basic book on people management ever written. Even better, it is a short and easy read.

***SPIN Selling* by Neil Rackham (McGraw-Hill, 1988)**
The original text on solution selling. All the concepts are just as valid today for business-to-business solution selling.

***Sun Tzu: The Art of War for Managers* by Gerald Michaelson (Adams Media, 2001)**
Sun Tzu first wrote *The Art of War* in 500 B.C. in warlord-dominated China; its thirteen chapters relate to the waging of war. This helpful book relates these strategies and principles to the waging of business.

***The Tipping Point* by Malcolm Gladwell (Little, Brown, 2000)**
In some ways, this book has little directly to do with marketing; in others, it has *everything* to do with marketing. We rank this as one of the most influential business books we've read in the last ten years. There is significant, low-cost marketing leverage here.

The Bootstrapper Aptitude Test

The following multiple-choice test will help you determine if you are a natural Bootstrapper:

1. When starting a business, what should you do first?
   a. Write a business plan and then try to raise money.
   b. Call lots of people to help you understand the issues in your market.
   c. Develop a prototype of your product idea.
   d. Hire a marketing consultant.

2. You have an idea. What should you do next?
   a. Implement the business plan.
   b. Rent office space and buy used office furniture.
   c. File for a patent.
   d. Fax your idea to 300 people and then call each one.

3. If you know you have a good product idea, what should you do next?
   a. Find a good intellectual property lawyer to protect your idea.
   b. Build a prototype and personally start selling it.
   c. Try to raise money.
   d. Hire a salesperson to sell your product.

4. You find someone who is interested in your product or service. You should:
   a. Explain that you would like to have her join your beta test program.
   b. Try to get her to place an order.
   c. Tell her you don't have the product available yet.
   d. Tell her all about the features you are going to add to the product.

5. Someone wants to buy your product, but he needs it to do a few more things in addition to its current capabilities. You should:
    a. Tell him it won't do those things.
    b. Get him to pay for the enhancements.
    c. Take the order and tell him it will ship in four weeks.
    d. Explain why those things are difficult to do and convince him to buy the current product.

6. A major publication calls saying it is writing a big article about your product and wants you to buy an ad in the same issue of its magazine. You have enough money for the ad, but not much more. You should:
    a. Buy the ad.
    b. Tell the caller your advertising budget is already committed.
    c. Tell the caller you don't have enough money.
    d. Tell the caller to get lost.

7. You're still just getting started and Dun & Bradstreet calls asking for company information and detailed financial data. You should:
    a. Give the information.
    b. Politely decline.
    c. Refer D & B to your accountant.
    d. Don't return the call.

8. A major potential customer says she wants to fly to visit you, but you're still working out of your house. You should:
    a. Tell her you are just getting started and don't have an office that will accommodate a visit.
    b. Rent office space prior to the visit and get your family and friends to occupy all the desks.

   c. Tell her you will be traveling the week she wants to visit.
   d. Borrow your accountant's office and hang your shingle over his the day of the visit.

9. You're the only person working full-time in the business and you're asked how many employees you have. Say:
   a. We have 50 employees.
   b. We have 20 employees.
   c. I'm the only one.
   d. We have six people involved in the business.

10. You've just made your first sale and generated your first monthly profit. You should:
   a. Give yourself a raise.
   b. Get that bigger office you have wanted.
   c. Throw a party.
   d. Hire a consultant.

Answers:

Question   #1: b
Question   #2: d
Question   #3: b
Question   #4: b
Question   #5: b or c
Question   #6: b
Question   #7: b
Question   #8: a
Question   #9: d (those involved includes spouse, accountant,
                    printer, lawyer, insurance agent, and yourself)
Question #10: c (and enjoy it!)

Score Yourself:

0 to 2 correct
You are a natural bureaucrat—you might consider running for public office, but not running a Bootstrapped business.

3 to 5 correct
You might want to look for a big company as your natural home.

6 to 8 correct
Find a mentor in Bootstrapping before going any further.

9 to 10 correct
You are a natural Bootstrapper—"You've got what it takes."

INDEX

A

accountants, 49–50
accounts payable, 92
accounts receivable
  vs. cash, 83
  managing your, 89–95
advertising, 113
advisory boards, 107, 110
Alcantra, Marcia, 22
analysts, 7, 10
aptitude test, 219–222
Aromasys Inc., 46–47, 56–57
Art of War, The (Tzu),
  206–207
assets, 70, 72
Auguste, Donna, 158

B

balance sheets, 70–72
bartering, 55, 58
book value, 72
Bootstrapper Aptitude Test,
  219–222
Bootstrapping
  advantages of, xx–xxii
  attraction of, xix
  defined, xv

strategies for successful,
  3–15
Bottom-Up Marketing (Reis
  and Trout), 217
Bragg, Marcus, 52, 66
broadband, ix, xi
brochures, 52
business
  buying an existing,
    11–12
  changing direction of,
    104–105
  checklist for starting,
    215–216
  competition, 206–209
  differentiating your, 36–38
  expansion of, 211–212
  incremental growth of,
    99–100
  maturation of, 212–214
  simplification of, 10
  thinking big for, 101
business awards, 145
Business by the Book (Burkett),
  217
business cards, 126–128
business measures, 211
business partners, 12–14, 53

business problems
    alternate solutions to,
        45–58
    See also crises

C

capital equipment, 70
Carstenssen, Susan, 192
cash, vs. invoices, 83
cash flow forecasts, 77–83,
    211
cash flow statements, 76–77
cash management, 69–70
    cash flow forecasts,
        77–83
    debt collection and, 89–95
    decreasing expenses and,
        84–85
    financial statements for,
        70–77
    increasing cash collection
        and, 84
    planning horizon for, 80
charitable work, 162–163
communication skills, 38–40
competition, dealing with
    bigger, 206–209
consultants, 7, 10, 49–50
cost savings, 59–67, 84–85
credit, obtaining, 96–97
crises
    alternate solutions to,
        45–58
    coping with, 108–109

lessons learned from,
    149–150
customer education, 189
customer events, 197
customers
    dealing with problems of,
        192–195
    expectations of, 195
    feedback from, 1–2, 6–7,
        18–21, 23–24, 196
    keeping promises to,
        193–194
    listening to, 38–40, 194
    "Love Letters" from,
        196–197
    market testing with,
        103–104
    objections from, 26
    reference, 24–25, 51,
        205–206
    researching, 33–34
    rewarding best, 116–117
    satisfying, 155–156
    staying loyal to earliest,
        120–121, 197
    understanding needs of,
        34–35
customer satisfaction surveys,
    195
customer service
    building loyalty through,
        192
    importance of, 187–189
    rules for quality,
        201–203

tips for, 192–197
user conferences and,
197–199

D
deadlines, 154–155
debt collection, 89–95
decision making, clarity in,
10
Dell Computer, xix
discounts
asking for, 66–67
offering, for quicker
payments, 84, 94
Doan, Lurita, xvi, 8–9

E
eBags, 10–11, 108–109
egos, 159–160
e-mail, 160–161
employees
to avoid, 174–175
delegating tasks to, 154
efficient, 180–181
emphasizing thriftiness
with, 59–60
empowering, 183
from existing businesses,
12
finding, 65, 169–171
finding specialists,
173–174
hiring first, 168

interviewing potential,
176–178
likeability of, 165
matching, to right job, 181
meetings with, 182–183
qualities needed in,
168–169, 175–176
quality of, 165–167
retaining, 182–185
salaries for, 66
socializing with, 157
training, 179–180
wants of, 185
when to start hiring,
171–173
endorsements, 206
equipment
capital, 70
used, 53–54, 62
exercise, 151
exhibitions, 124–126
existing businesses, 11–12
expenses, reducing, 59–67,
84–85
experts, 7, 10
external funding, xx–xxi

F
Fall of Advertising and the Rise
of PR (Reis and Reis), 217
Fanuzzi, John, 74–75,
86–87
Field, Andrew, xvii, 4–5, 132,
189

financial setbacks, 10–11
financial statements, 70–83
 balance sheets, 70–72
 cash flow forecasts, 77–83
 cash flow statements, 76–77
 income statements, 72–73
financing, obtaining, 96–97
focus, keeping your, 153–154
free trials, 23–24, 206

G
Gianforte, Greg, xx, 18–19
Golden Ratio Woodworks, 74–75, 86–87
growth, incremental, 99–100

H
HDO Sports, 90, 96, 98, 119–120
herd mentality, 54
high-margin opportunities, 3, 6
hiring process
 interviews, 176–178
 review stage of, 178–179
 See also employees
home offices, 60–61
human interest magazines, 147

I
iClick Technologies, 104–105, 142–143, 200

income statements, 72–73
Innovation and Entrepreneurship (Drucker), 217
innovations, market testing, 103–104
innovative thinking, 45, 48, 54, 214
interview process, 176–178
inventory, 211
invoices
 vs. cash, 83
 See also accounts receivable
Irizarry, Rob, 187–188, 193–194
IT systems, 62

J
Jenkins, Tim, xvii, 162–163, 166–167
journalists
 additional contacts for, 139–140
 contacting, 130–137
 providing information to, 144–145
 See also media coverage

L
Lahoud, Joseph, xvii, 161–162
late payment excuses, 95
lawyers, 49–50

LC Technologies, 161–162
leadership
   from Bootstrapping to,
      212–214
   by example, 106–107
Les Schwab Tires, 190–191
liabilities, 70, 72
listening skills, 38–40
Littlefield, Darran, 92, 93,
   94

M

margins, high, 3, 6, 105–106
marketing
   brochures, 52
   business cards and,
      126–128
   co-op funding for, 51
   day-to-day, 119
   of differentiators, 115
   online, 121–124
   purpose of, 111–112
   rules for, 113–122
   of single message, 114
   social network, 118–119
   strategy, 128
   at trade shows, 124–126
   VIP endorsements and,
      119–120
marketing agencies, 51
market research
   conventional, 112–113
   using sales as, 18–21
market testing, 103–104

McGowan, Lon, xvi, 114–
   115, 142–143, 172, 200
McLean-Foreman, Alasdair,
   90, 96, 98, 119–120
media
   learning about the, 131,
      133
   trade press, 133–134
media coverage, 129–147
   of awards events, 145
   expert speakers and,
      140–141, 144–145
   feature articles, 138–140
   indirect opportunities for,
      146–147
   journalists and, 130–137
   newspapers, 134–137
   photos for, 137–138
   staged stunts for, 140,
      142–143
   using, 145–146
meetings, company,
   182–183
Meltzer, Brady, 32, 168, 192
Microsoft, xix
money, importance of saving,
   59–67
money-back guarantees,
   205–206
money management. *See* cash
   management
money shortages, 10–11
motivation, 152
Murphy, Sean, xvii, 50–51,
   55, 64–65, 66

N

Nash, Scott, 102
National Federation of
     Independent Business
     (NFIB), xix, xviii
New Technology
     Management, Inc., 9
niche, finding a, 35–36
Nordmark, Jon, xvii, xxi,
     10–11, 60, 108–109

O

office environment
     creating an efficient,
          180–181
     creating fun, 158
     image and, 60–61
One Minute Manager, The
     (Blanchard and Johnson),
     217
online marketing, 121–124
open-source software, 62
opportunities, discovering,
     6–7
Optimus Inc., 50–55,
     64–65

P

partners, 12–14, 53
Peltier, Mark, xvii, 46–47,
     56–57
perspective, keeping problems
     in, 156–157

phone bills, 63
phone systems, 63
pilot implementations,
     40–41
Point B Solutions, 91–93,
     162–163, 166–167
Potter, Sandy, 51
pre-selling, 18–19, 20–21
press coverage, 129–147
prices, refusing to lower,
     105–106
Prime Valet Cleaners,
     113–119, 115
PrintingForLess.com, 4–5,
     132, 189
problems
     confronting, 152–153
     dealing with customers',
          192–195
     keeping in perspective,
          156–157
     not taking personally,
          158–159
     thinking through, 152
product development,
     customer input and, 1–3,
     6–7, 15, 18–24
product differentiation,
     36–38, 115
product endorsements,
     119–120
products
     benefit of not having, 2–3
     changing direction of,
          104–105

communicating value of,
209–210
endorsements for, 206
finding right, 3, 6
giving away, 23–24, 206
high margins on, 105–106
market testing, 103–104
pre-selling, 18–21
timing of, 100–101
professional fees, 49–50
profit-and-loss statements,
72–73
prospecting, time for, 43–44
prospects
sales calls to, 38–40
See also customers; sales

R

receivables, managing your,
89–95
reference customers, 24–25,
51, 205–206
rejection, 26–27
return on investment (ROI),
209–210
RightNow Technologies
free trials by, 23–24
IT system of, 62
online marketing by, 122–
124
pilot implementations by,
40–41
pre-selling at, 18–19
recruitment at, 184

sales at, 25
sales trips at, 52–53

S

sales
asking tough questions and,
41
communicating value and,
209–210
communication skills and,
38–40
difficulty of, 27–28, 32–33
focusing on, 17, 20, 28–29
as market research, 18–21,
23
not delegating, 106
personalizing, 25
pitfalls to avoid in, 43–44
positive attitude for,
208–209
as priority, 21
repeat, 42
right attitude toward, 33
steps for making first,
33–42
sales obstacles, 26–27
salespersons
hiring first, 168
performance of, 106–107
salaries for, 66
training, 179–180
See also employees
sales profession, 31–32
sales trips, 52–53

Schwab, Les, 190–191
Scurry, Kim, 122–123
service, finding right, 3, 6
small businesses, xviii
socializing, with staff, 157
social networks, 118–119
solutions, finding creative,
   45–58
speeches, 140–141, 144–145
SPIN Selling (Rackham), 218
staff. *See* employees
stress
   lessons learned from,
     149–150
   strategies for minimizing,
     150–163
Sun Tzu (Michaelson), 218
Szydlowski, Paul, xvii–xviii,
   11–12, 113–119

T
tasks, delegating, 154
thriftiness, 59–67
timing, 100–101
Tipping Point (Gladwell), 218
to-do lists, 160
trade press, 133–134
trade shows, 124–126

U
user conferences, 197–199

V
value, communicating, 209–
   210
vendors, discounts from,
   66–67
venture capitalists, xx-xxi, 54
video desktop conferencing, x

W
Web sites, 121–122

X
Xperts, 158